BEAUTIFULLY
BROKEN

Bobbi Jo Reed

RECOMMENDATIONS

Helping with the Healing House ministry has changed my life forever. Bobbi Jo's strength, hope, and experience in recovery is like none I have ever known. She has changed the lives of countless individuals, their families and the community.
Tom Langhofer, General Manager
Rodrock Development

Bobbi Jo Reed is a living testament to the prevailing notion that through the grace of Jesus Christ, the worst thing is never the last thing. Bobbi Jo's is a story that underscores God's healing, redemption and hope, and by God's unsearchable grace she has paved the way for community transformation through her vision and leadership at the Healing House.
Rev. Scott Chrostek, Campus Pastor
Church of the Resurrection, Kansas City, MO

I have been privileged to know Bobbi Jo and watch her continue to triumph over addictions to oversee wonderful spiritual homes for women and men with similar pasts. UMB BANK was honored to be asked to finance houses on Saint John Avenue that would become homes for people who wanted to change their lives in a faith based environment.
Robert Harr, Senior Vice President
UMB BANK

CONTENTS

FOREWARD

Acknowledgments

About Healing House

About the Author

FOREWARD

Luke 7 tells the story of Jesus as a dinner guest at the home of a Pharisee named Simon. Undoubtedly many respected members of the community who were Simon's friends joined them for this meal. Part way through the meal a woman barged into the dining room. This by itself would have been surprising and, depending upon the setting, inappropriate. But this woman was, the text explains, "a sinner" – a euphemism for prostitute.

One can imagine Simon's shock and embarrassment.

The woman saw Jesus reclining at the table and made her way to him, weeping as she stood behind him, her tears falling to his feet. In her hands was an alabaster flask of costly scented oil. The woman knelt at Jesus' feet, let down her hair, wiped her tears from his feet, then anointed them with fragrant oil.

Why did the woman come to Simon's house to find Jesus? Luke doesn't tell us, but I imagine that earlier in the day as Jesus entered the town, he had a momentary encounter with her as she stood in the crowd watching him. As his eyes met hers, she quickly averted her gaze. Yet in that moment, she felt as if he knew everything there was to know about her. I imagine Jesus calling her by name and saying, "You matter to God. He loves you dearly. Come and follow me." That night she brought the most precious thing she had, an alabaster jar filled with costly scented oil, and she offered it and herself to Christ.

When I think of Bobbi Jo Reed I think of this woman in Luke. Hers is one of the most powerful redemption stories I know.

Bobbi Jo found in Jesus one who loved her and showed her grace and mercy. She discovered that God is the God of restoration and second chances. As she trusted in Christ her life was transformed. She truly became a "new creature in Christ."

But Bobbi Jo didn't stop with accepting the grace of God. She understood that this grace came with an expectation and a calling. She heard the call of God to help other women and men who society may have considered hopeless causes. She knew if offered an opportunity to respond to Christ's love, their lives could be changed as hers was. She brought her alabaster jar of costly perfume – the inheritance you'll read about in this book – and offered it to Christ, purchasing the Healing House's first home.

I know few leaders with the vision, passion and love that I see in Bobbi Jo. God has used her to fulfill Jesus self-described mission to "seek and to save those who are lost."

I have the joy of serving as one of the pastors of the women and men who are a part of the Healing House. I've been blessed by listening to their testimonies, baptizing their babies and welcoming them into the membership of the church. Each is a living, breathing witness to the power of God to transform lives.

This story bears powerful witness to the gospel. It will touch your heart and inspire you to follow in the footsteps of Jesus, who saw in the sinners and tax collectors of his day people who mattered to God.

Adam Hamilton
Senior Pastor
The United Methodist Church of the Resurrection

CHAPTER ONE

UNREPAIRABLE?

The hardest part of this story is beginning it.

If I could just introduce the woman you see today, we'd be fine. *I'd jump right in.*

"Hi. I'm Bobbi Jo Reed, founder and director of a Christian recovery ministry that offers residential treatment to alcoholics and drug addicts."

You'd smile, while wondering to yourself why someone would ever choose work like *that,* and we'd be off and running.

But even as I'd say those words of introduction, I'd know how much I want you to know the rest of the story, what I call the *real* introduction to Bobbi Jo Reed.

Sometimes that real introduction gets boiled down to a bunch of horrific facts about my life:

- 24 broken bones
- 16 rapes I can remember, not counting the time I spent as a prostitute or imprisoned as a sex slave
- 2 abortions
- 1 stint of homelessness, sleeping on an asphalt parking lot under a semi-trailer.

But these facts are just half my story.

The other half, the important half, the half that matters, began when a 37-year-old woman dying in alcohol and drug addiction encountered Jesus Christ, and was *loved* into a whole new life that allowed her to help bring life to others who were just as lost.

You may be one of the middle-class business people who saw me passed out drunk on the cold asphalt of that parking lot. I don't know if you felt compassion or curiosity, but you most certainly felt hopelessness. You may have asked yourself, *how could someone who has gone so low ever be saved?*

Or you may have been me – or you *are* me – lost in addiction and hopelessness, looking at yourself and wondering *how could someone who has gone so low ever be saved.*

Or you may have a family member or loved one who right now is me, living in frightening conditions, and trapped by choices that lead to greater and greater darkness. And you wrestle against hopelessness, wondering *how someone who has gone so low could ever be saved.*

My story is for all of you, because my Savior is for all of us. God's redeeming power found a woman who wasn't searching for Him; indeed, who didn't even know He could be her way out. When He found me, He re-grew my life from the bottom up, and from the inside out.

Please allow my story to reawaken hope in you.

If Bobbi Jo Reed could be saved, God can save anyone.

And He does.

And He will.

CHAPTER TWO

BEGINNING TO BREAK

My dreams never centered on becoming an alcoholic, or a prostitute, or a drug addict.

If you had asked me at five what I wanted to be, I would have picked a bleached blonde like Goldie Hawn or Farrah Fawcett. That was me, a TV-watching Kansas City kid with two big brothers, a dad who was a police officer for the city, a mom who stayed home to take care of us in our two-bedroom bungalow, and a Pekinese dog named Ching Tai Lee.

If you'd watched us from afar, we looked a little like the Cleavers. Sometimes we'd wake up to Mom dancing as Aretha Franklin blared in the background. She read the classics to us before naptime and organized family camping trips to the Ozarks and visits to our grandparents. She was a Cub Scout leader for my brothers, and helped with my Brownie troop. Many afternoons she'd retrieve us from romps in the woods behind our house by calling, "Lucy LaGoose (that's 'I Love Lucy' to the uninitiated) is on TV!"

And those woods! We'd build forts with the neighbor kids, and use the pack of Kools we stole from our mom's stash to experiment with smoking cigarettes. We'd also nervously look through a Playboy magazine or two left behind by the bigger kids, but we didn't get what the fuss was – all those naked people looked pretty gross to us.

Neighbors would have praised my dad's protectiveness. When race riots were exploding in the late 60's and Dad learned the Black Panthers were targeting police officers' houses, he moved us to Piper, Kansas for the summer to live in a pop-up camper so we'd be out of harm's way. Those who knew about his early years would have told you he worked long hours to be sure we didn't go without like he had, growing up in a fatherless family with six kids so mired in poverty they had to stuff cardboard inside their worn-out shoes to keep out the snow and cold.

My dad? He wasn't going to see his family live poor. And my mom? People said she was a looker and worked hard to keep herself up. All-around, a nice family. Yep, that's what the neighbors said – because that's all they saw.

The family no one knew

Behind this made-for-TV story, we lived out another reality.

My dad seemed to be always working; I remember standing alone at the six-pane window at the front of the house watching for him, longing for him to come home. Later I would learn some of these absences happened because he simply didn't want to be at home. I can remember more than one episode when he packed his bags to leave – even now I can recall the sounds of all of us crying and begging him to stay.

Behind her "everything is wonderful" exterior, my mom tried to escape her loneliness and frustration with what would later become an addiction to prescription drugs. First it was diet pills – amphetamines – and then later a doctor-supplied combination of speed and Valium.

When her rage at a life of isolation with three small children (who came in just four years) would ignite an already drug-shortened fuse, she'd explode in screams and curses, then swing at us with whatever was close at hand, a curtain rod, or a belt. When we could, we'd head for the woods behind the house and hope her fury would pass.

On some level, I don't know that it occurred to us that life in other houses was much different from this. My mother told us stories about her mother punishing her disobedience by locking her in a dirt-floor root cellar, warning her of snakes and spiders there, then leaving the little girl alone in a terror-filled darkness. We were screamed at, cursed and sometimes hit, but no one ever locked us in a pit-black cellar. Maybe things at our house weren't that bad.

By age six I was expected to do laundry because Mom had gone somewhere to get help for something they told us was a "nervous breakdown." When Mom came home she was moody and withdrawn, so I washed clothes, and we three kids made do as we could.

In the muddle of these foggy years, there were issues small children just couldn't manage. My brother went for years with undiagnosed inner ear deafness, and as a result didn't speak correctly because he couldn't hear how words were supposed to sound. Since I learned to speak by imitating him, I, too, had a speech impediment. Also, because I was chubby and not quick at learning, there was little incentive for teachers to want to invest in me. School became an endurance test, redeemed only by recess. (Report cards showed poor scholastic progress, but I always got great marks on "plays well with others.")

Little by little, Mom came back to managing the house, making our lunches, and keeping things a little more predictable. And when I turned ten, it appeared me that life was about to improve considerably. We were moving to the suburbs to a three-bedroom house, so I'd have my own room. I felt like a princess! The bedroom, along with two bathrooms and a recreation room in the basement – it was a mansion. I made some friends quicker than I expected, and began to wonder if that move had actually moved us away from a whole lot of unhappiness to a land of hope.

The world does a 180°

When I hit seventh grade, hope of "normal" faded.

My dad had a heart attack, and though he recovered fairly quickly, life at our house would never be the same. Mom responded to a new fear of financial vulnerability by enrolling in college, training to be a recreational therapist. She threw herself into her schoolwork, but at home, she shut down...no cleaning the house, doing laundry, regular cooking or being part of family life.

Dad handled the fear differently. He'd always worked several jobs, first as a police officer, then with additional night jobs as a security officer at places like Wal-Mart and Woolco. Now, it seemed important we kids start working, too. He'd grown up in poverty, so working young and working hard looked to him like some protection for us against something similar happening.

So, he got jobs for my brothers and me at Save-On, the discount store where he was working nights. He'd pick us up after school; we'd often work until 9 at night, plus Saturday and all day Sunday. At age 12, I was going to school, and often working thirty-plus hours per week.

One of my brothers worked in the shoe department, the other in records – and then on the "ramp" where novelties were sold, like velvet pictures of Jesus knocking on the door, and those stand-up punch balloons. I worked in a storage room washing and sorting dishes to sell in house wares. The owner had acquired a whole barn full of restaurant dishes that were my domain. I'd get a grocery cart and put two 5-gallon buckets in it, then roll it across the store to a storage area to load it, then roll it back to my storeroom to wash and separate those dishes into sets.

Fortunately or unfortunately, depending on your view, I wasn't alone. The store had a pet department, so my nightly companion was a foul little monkey who spent most of his time masturbating – interesting entertainment for an uninformed 12-year-old girl.

At the time, this outward and work-focused life gave a great distraction from the weirdness we called home. When a seventh-grader goes to school all week, then works an adult job many nights and weekends, there's no much time to think. Or to feel. Or to question. Or to miss what girls at school talked about, like dance lessons, or baseball games, or TV shows. We came home weary, and got up the next day to do it again.

New friends – and an evil enemy – take over my life

I must have done fairly well on dish-sorting duty; before long I was promoted out of the storeroom to the candy counter out front. This step up brought with it a step out – a couple of the older girls who worked there took a liking to me, and one weekend invited me for pizza, and for a weekend sleepover. I was delighted. An invite from two 18-year-olds looked like world-class glamour to a chubby, awkward 12-year-old. My parents consented; not having me around for a weekend while our family was in such chaos removed one responsibility from a situation where no one wanted to be responsible anyway, so it looked like everyone was winning.

Little did any of us know that weekend would launch me onto a very dark, very destructive path that would steal the next 22 years of my life.

It started with a drink.

Introducing a pre-teen alcohol virgin to the party life looked like fun to these older girls, so for the first time in my life, I got drunk.

Maybe I'd had a sip of alcohol before, but it wasn't part of our lives. My dad wasn't much of a drinker, and my mom didn't drink much at the house, so it was something I wasn't aware of, either positively or negatively.

Ah, but that weekend changed all that. My first beer started a love affair. I'd been chubby my whole life, struggling with a speech impediment, neither smart or attractive, or worthy, really of much at all. Yet with the addition of just a little alcohol, all of a sudden I felt ten feet tall and bulletproof...funny, smart, sexy (as sexy as a 12-year-old could be)...I had arrived and I couldn't wait to get my hands on more of this.

I started hanging out with these friends every weekend. My friends helped me wrangle an ID from my cousin Marsha, who with her black hair and brown eyes looked nothing like me, but it got me into the discos and clubs and all the rest followed. I dated bouncers, danced 'til dawn, and was soon smoking weed and doing speed. The storeroom dishwasher whose best friend was a nasty monkey was now partying with the best of them. It came so fast, and so easily, it seemed to me. What had been empty felt filled.

The first time I knew I needed a drink, I was 13. My bouncer boyfriend had just dumped me when he discovered how old I was; I was as devastated as only a barely-teenage girl with a first broken heart could be. But instead of the normal teen-girl scenario of crying myself to sleep, I sent someone to the liquor store next to Save-On to buy booze, and chugged a six-pack on my break.

Some invisible line got crossed that night. They say the time in life when you begin serious drinking is also the place where emotional maturing stops. For me, it was 13, so for the next couple of decades I lived in a woman's body, making a woman's choices, with the dangerously immature emotional capacity of a little girl.

High school businesswoman

No one does high school as deeply under the influence as I was and succeeds. I was sleeping in classes, disconnected, and failing most everything. Everything, that is, but lunch hour. When the bell would ring signaling lunch, I'd head straight for the girls' bathroom, and spend the next 40 minutes dealing speed, and later THC, a hallucinogenic powder. Of course if you'd asked me if I was a drug dealer, I'd have flatly denied it. In my mind, I had just found a way to turn enough cash to support my habit. Kind of responsible and self-reliant, if you wanted to see it that way.

At home, the life I'd created of disappearing on weekends to drink and drug with my friends worked fairly well for everyone. Dad was gone most of the time; Mom was still shut down in depression. Both my brothers were partying, but neither went as deeply into the party life as I did, and neither created the uproar I could at home. When my parents asked too many questions, or said no to something I wanted, I'd throw a stinking fit like the ones I'd seen my mother perform when I was small – cursing, screaming, acting crazy. For my parents it was easier to give in and have me disappear for the weekend than do battle with a screaming banshee.

Bracing for the worst

A car accident when I was 15 brought me back home. On Halloween night, my drunk friend Lisa drove us off a bridge. The car rolled, flipped three times, and landed in a drainage ditch upside down.

My back was broken in three places, with three compressed fractures, and my neck was also fractured. I spent the next year in a metal body brace that came up under my armpits, with metal in the back to keep my spine straight, and a corset-front to hold it onto me. I had to drop out of school, of course, and it would have been the year from hell, except I was prescribed Librium, Darvoset and Valium three times a day. And I chased these drugs with large doses of beer, Miller ponies, and a good amount of Strawberry Hill wine. The year in that brace was a hazy, dopey, buzzy blur.

As soon as I could tolerate leaving the house, I strapped on that back brace and lumbered back to work and partying. Anything seemed better than being shut up with my mother day and night, even with the aid of all those drugs.

One night at a party, I was in a back room smoking weed and drinking with my crowd. I was spaced out enough not to notice, but a few at a time people began leaving the room, and I found myself alone with a guy I barely knew. He grabbed me, and started pulling at my clothes. Fighting was useless; I was still in the brace, so as soon as he threw me on the floor, I was as helpless as a turtle upside down on her shell. I cried and screamed for him to stop, but he didn't. When he finished, he got up, and went back out to the party.

It was exactly a week before my 16th birthday.

In the four years since alcohol and drugs took over my life, I lost most vestiges of any sense of what was moral. But for reasons I couldn't explain, it had seemed very important that I hang onto my virginity. I don't know where this idea originated; I don't recall anyone talking to me about this, and there was certainly no faith influence to direct me. But somewhere in my heart, I believed that sex should be special, and somehow it should be linked to love.

All this was swirling inside me as I rolled over and pushed myself up off that dirty floor. And in what I now see as a tragic attempt to try to make it right, I went out to the party and approached my rapist. "Uh…you're going to be my boyfriend now, right?" I pleaded haltingly. Then I offered him my phone number. As he turned away, I stumbled off, but I honestly thought, "Surely he will call me because of what he just took from me."

There was no call.

A year later, I was raped again, this time by two boys I considered "good friends." But a month after the rapes, my period didn't come.

When I finally told my mom what had happened, she didn't ask who did this to me. She didn't rage, or sympathize, or cry, or wonder if I should get counseling or talk to my police officer father about an arrest.

"I will arrange for an abortion," she said without emotion. "We won't speak about this again."

I went to the clinic high on Quaaludes. In the waiting room, they provided all of us with 10 grams of Valium, "to take the edge off…" they told us. Most of the little housewives who were waiting with me didn't know what to do with their Valiums, so I collected them and took them in a handful, along with another Quaalude. Even though I was off-the-charts drugged, the abortion was awful, excruciating pain. My heart felt pain, too, even through the fog, because even with no one telling me, I knew it was wrong.

My brother picked me up from the clinic; I smoked a bowl of weed on the way back home. Though my mom saw me come in, not a word was said about what had just happened.

I went straight to my room, shut the door and drank myself unconscious.

CHAPTER THREE

TEN YEARS ON THE EDGE

Here's what I'd like to be the story of the ten years of my life from 17-27:

"Deeply scared and lonely teen-age girl gets raped by a stranger at a drug party. As a result, her parents learn she's spent the last four years covering up a weekend life of partying, fueled by alcohol and drugs. The reality of the rape and an abortion after another rape forces the three of them to admit this police officer's daughter is in deep trouble. With courage and love, they seek out treatment. The daughter gets clean, the family gets healthier, and the next ten years are filled with happiness for everyone."

Unfortunately, this book isn't a fairy tale.

High on pizza?

The rape and abortion were now a fuzzy memory I squashed down as best I could.

I had already quit school following the back injury, so when I had recovered well enough to work again, I got a job at a pizza heaven for druggies. Now there was no need to hold back from getting smashed in order to go to work; at that pizza place, we meshed the two seamlessly. I'd smoke weed with the manager out in the parking lot in his car between orders. Then, as soon as the shop would close for the night, we'd bake up some Magic Mushroom pizzas, big combos loaded with hallucinogens, then wash them down with keg beer as we partied into the night.

This party-intensity proved to be great therapy, because just after the abortion, my back brace had been removed, and with it all my painkillers. As a result, I shook all the time and had taken to starting the day with whiskey, not for the taste, but because I couldn't function without it.

You'd think my police officer dad would have some awareness of what was happening with his daughter. But he had his own issues: my mother's withdrawal from life meant the house was atrocious, so he'd spend his day off shoveling out as he could, and cleaning up dishes that had stacked up for a week. From his view, he likely had his hands full without thinking about a hellion daughter who made life at home miserable whenever she chose to crash there.

To cosmetology school

Somehow between the pizza highs and the whiskey lows, I managed to get my GED and enroll in cosmetology school. My parents paid for the venture; besides hopes for a new start, this new direction gave a positive story my mother could tell her friends – and introduced me to a cool, new set of friends.

The girls I met at school hung out with bad boy bikers from a town an hour away. The police were clearly scared of us, so left us alone as we partied and generally raised hell. I'd hang with these new friends all I could, dressed like a Biker Chick, did cocaine, and then worked to fund my binges by selling drugs.

Amazingly, I successfully finished cosmetology school. My mom bragged about it to her friends, adding that I was now working not one, but three jobs, and had found love with a responsible guy who worked as a roofer.

Working girl

I was indeed working three jobs, and the daytime segment did involve fixing hair. At the second job I cleaned an apartment building; the third involved working as the assistant night manager at a small jewelry store my dad owned as an investment.

But the jewelry store job wasn't just an innocent income source. My dad as owner meant I could drink on the job. (Who is going to tell on the owner's daughter?) Plus, my dad's partner did drugs, and I soon discovered he kept a stash of speed nicely organized in the little jewelry repair box compartments. So, when I augmented his supply with Black Beauties and Christmas Trees, we were able to quite neatly and discreetly fill up the jewelry drawers with a healthy store of amphetamines.

And the boyfriend? Actually, we had the party house, a three-bedroom apartment with me, Roofer Ralph, and two other guys. To be sure we could always keep up the party pace, we kept a keg of beer on tap in the dining room.

At one point, I left town for a few weeks to follow Roofer Ralph to a job in Louisiana, and of course no one cleaned while I was gone. The shag carpet in the dining room was always moist because of dripping and spills from the ever-present keg, so when I returned, I found pot plants growing out of the shag carpet! I didn't know if cleaning should require a vacuum or a weed whacker.

The roof(er) caves in...on me

One night after an entire day of drinking when I'd passed out in a bar and had to be carried home to our apartment, my roofer staggered in about 1:00 a.m. I'd slept off enough of the drunk to be irritated that he was partying without me, and I demanded to know where he'd been.

This is not the question to ask a violent, drunken man who pounded hammers for a living. He ripped off my nightgown and started punching me – a 6'5" man pummeling a 5'4" woman – I knew I was in big trouble. So I wiggled myself out of his grasp and ran naked from the apartment to the home of friends in another part of the complex. As they opened the door to me, the phone rang and my friend Bernie told the roofer, "Yeah, she's right here. And she's naked. What's going on?"

"Nothing...you know how crazy she gets when she's high," Roofer Ralph answered. "I'll be right over to get her."

I turned and ran, then crouched down behind the bushes next to the apartment building. I stayed there in the cold as long as I could, but I knew I wouldn't make it through the night. Now I had no hope my friends would help; there was no other way out but to go back to the apartment and hope the roofer had gone to sleep. Maybe I could slip in, get some clothes, and call my family to rescue me...

The plan appeared to be working, but just as my brother answered his phone, Ralph woke up, grabbed the phone, and started beating me in the head with it. I managed to cry out, "Help me..."

By the time my brother arrived, I had sustained three broken ribs, and such severe bruising on the front of my breasts and stomach that there was no white skin left.

The doctor who treated me took one look and said, "You need to tell me who did this to you because he should be in prison..." However, I insisted I fell down a flight of stairs.

And as soon as I'd healed a little, I moved back in with the roofer. Surely he hadn't meant it. Maybe I'd done something to set him off. I loved him, after all, and doesn't love mean giving second chances?

The relationship finally ended when he tried to kill me by beating my head again and again into the frame of our water-bed. I made it out alive only because our other two roommates happened in and stopped him.

"Bobbi Jo has the worst luck..."

I ran back to my parents, as I did repeatedly, until I healed.

My mother worked hard to come up with believable stories to explain what I was doing at home. If you'd asked her friends, they'd say I had some version of the flu for nearly 22 years!

But as soon as the worst of the bruising disappeared, Mom would insist I do my hair and get my nails done. Even though I was high on alcohol and drugs, as long as I looked good to her friends, I met her expectations. Appearances were what mattered. Looking good provided a shield from the pain of life, just as substance abuse and bizarre, sickly imitations of love provided a shield from pain for me.

Next, secretarial school

Even after this ugly ending to my relationship with the roofer, my parents stayed committed to help me. We decided together a different work setting might help me turn over a new leaf. This time my parents paid tuition for training in secretarial skills.

In the next few years it appeared to the family I was straightening out. They knew I worked in the office of a radiator company, then in customer service at Wal-Mart.

The rest of the story was far less rosy. At the radiator company everyone drank, both during and after the workday, and company-funded dinners quickly degenerated into sloshy, drunken parties. Unfortunately I was better at drinking than I was at showing up for work, and at last got fired.

I moved to Wal-Mart, but lost my job there, too, for coming to work drunk.

Since I didn't live at home during these years, my parents had little picture of how totally dysfunctional my love life had become. For example, they knew I was living with a man and his two children. They didn't know he had chosen me so I could take care of his kids while he was out getting high.

Sometimes I'd need to call home for a rescue following a beating, or an arrest after a drunken, drugged-out party. However, a real rescue would mean I'd have to want to leave the life I was living, and by now I wasn't at all sure I wanted a different life.

Now, a thief

With the help of all this drinking, I moved toward the end of my twenties unable to hold a job, a serious problem for a woman trying to support alcohol and drug habits. So, in a spirit of entrepreneurship, a boyfriend and I headed to

Leavenworth to commit home burglaries. Though I didn't actually do the break-ins, I'd drive the get-away car so after a heist we could unload the stuff to a fence who'd supply us with alcohol in payment.

Until now, I'd escaped punishment for an amazing amount of wrong doing by telling the arresting officer about my dad, the long-time Kansas City police officer. Of course occasionally I'd come across a highway patrolman who'd respond, "I don't give a damn who your dad is; you are going to jail!" But Dad would retain an attorney and I'd usually go free.

However, my luck with the law was about to run out.

During one of these break-ins, the homeowner came home, and wrote down my license tags. Unfortunately, the car was registered in both my name and my dad's. The next day, detectives went to talk to Officer Reed about his whereabouts the night before. When he confronted me, I tried to lie my way out of it, but this time he had proof.

A crack in the wall of denial

After nearly ten years of non-stop drinking and drugging, and showing up bloody and broken at my parents' home, this on-the-books criminal act finally pushed my dad to act.

I was going into treatment.

We started close to home, a detox facility downtown in Kansas City, Kansas. A bunch of very sick-looking men milled around the detox area; only a sheet hung from the ceiling separated them from what was called the "women's area." My dad took one look, and said, "You are not staying here..."

We headed for Choice #2 in Atchison, Kansas where a month in detox and treatment cost $3,000, a hefty sum for a police officer back in the '80's. But my dad had the court's assurance that if I completed this program, I'd get drug diversion instead of jail time, and if I completed probation I wouldn't have a criminal record.

The reality of leaving me at that old motel-turned-treatment, plus the 22 whiskey bottles he found under my bed at home marked my dad's first move from denial. It would no longer work to say, "That's just Bobbi Jo..." His daughter was trapped in the kind of trouble she wasn't going to ever outgrow.

CHAPTER FOUR

OVER THE EDGE

The next 18 months after treatment, I lived with my parents and stayed sober.

Well, "sober" may be a relative term.

Being without drugs and alcohol during treatment was a gruesome experience. So in the absence of these highs, I turned to another: I fell in love with Eric, the crackhead, who was also in treatment.

Once home, I tried following the treatment center's instructions, and headed to a 12-step meeting. But I threw up my hands after two meetings. "Just a bunch of pathetic old losers," I told Eric. "These people aren't drinking anymore because they can't; they are too old. I do not belong there!"

Though I stayed away from substance abuse for nearly two years, nothing in my thinking or my heart shifted. Treatment didn't "take" because I had no real intention to change; I went to avoid going to jail and to appease my parents. Never did I picture my life without drugs or alcohol; I was just looking for an escape from the consequences that might make the future harder for me.

In other words, I was a time bomb waiting to explode.

"My Crackhead in Shining Armor..."

My drug-of-choice, aka Eric, eventually became irresistible, so in time I left my parents and we moved in together. Not long after, he relapsed and became violent with me.

In one of our worst episodes, he came after me for hiding what I had intended to be the rent money inside a pillow. He needed cash for crack, so when I dove onto the bed in a futile attempt to protect the cash, he threw me back, and broke my leg against the waterbed frame.

My parents retrieved me, but as soon as I was healed enough to escape, I headed back to Eric's arms. What else could I do? I loved him!

When I got to our apartment, he was smoking crack. I sized up the situation, thought of the misery of the last couple of months without him, and in an instant flushed two years of sobriety down the toilet. If the choice was between Eric and living clean, I had to have Eric. "If you can't beat 'em, join 'em..." I told myself with a shrug and took a hit off his crack pipe.

I had done lots of cocaine, but this was a first encounter with crack, and it left me ready to jump out of my skin. Medication was the only answer, so I headed out for a liquor store for a big bottle of whiskey. Within a month I was drinking more than I ever had in my life...a quart to a half-gallon a day, along with regular encounters with crack.

Crack made Eric mean, and soon the drinking and drugs became painkillers for the beatings I was enduring. But the beatings were taking their toll. I chose to leave, but moved from Eric to relationships with equally vile men. For example, one of these boyfriends confessed he had been to prison for "accidentally" killing a man – by stabbing him 23 times. Some accident!

A slide to new depths

An addict without cash is an addict in trouble. Fortunately I stumbled over a new survival skill, something called Day Labor. If you'd show up at a location about 3:30 in the morning, people there might hire you to do one-off, often-miserable jobs. (Once I spent the day in a river, hauling stuff from train cars that had derailed). Day Labor fit my needs well: if I'd work a day, I could get enough money to drink for two or three days.

One morning I left the 3:30 a.m. show-up without work for the day, so I killed time until a nearby liquor store opened. There I met a couple of guys who invited me to head with them to Kansas City, Missouri to party. Can't work? Good day to drink, I thought.

The "party" – an orgy of drinking and drugging – went on for a couple of days. In a drill that had almost become commonplace, the guy I'd chosen decided I was flirting with others, and gave me a pounding. But this time there was a new, terrifying twist.

"You cheated on me," he snarled, "and now you owe me. You're going out to make me some money." It took me a moment to understand – he was sending me out to prostitute myself, to turn tricks. I was terrified, but because this 6'7" former pro ball player had already beaten me so badly, I was more terrified to refuse. He dumped me on the street between two liquor stores, and ordered me to not come back until I had money in my hand.

I've heard women say how powerful it made them feel to prostitute themselves, and I wondered what they were smoking to say such a thing. It was the most incomprehensibly demoralizing thing I had ever experienced, bar none. Voluntarily getting into a car with a complete stranger who could be planning to beat me, cut my throat, even kill me…even with my history of terrible moments with violent men, I was scared to death.

And this time, I was so humiliated I couldn't call family. This was beyond what even I would expect them to accept.

I did what I had to that day, but I hoped I had paid my dues for whatever crime I'd committed against the pimp. With the money I earned I bought lunchmeat, bread, whiskey and cigarettes, and brought my peace offering back to the party house.

It didn't earn my freedom.

We moved quickly from that house to a seedy hotel in downtown Kansas City, Missouri and I was sent to the streets every day to bring home money to support the pimp's crack addiction or endure some of the most brutal beatings I had ever experienced.

And I couldn't contrive a way to escape him. Because I was so ashamed of what I'd become, I felt I couldn't call my family for help. It seemed there was no way out this time.

At first I worried that someone I knew would see me. But the farther down this road I went, I became an "It," not a person. Who cared if someone saw me? This is what someone as worthless as me had to do to survive.

In the midst of this, I got disgustingly sick. I had Crohn's Disease, an inflammatory bowel disease that affected my intestines and usually caused stomach cramps and diarrhea. But untreated, it got worse so I developed pinholes inside my intestines that tunneled their way to the outside, making open lesions on my rectum.

All my pimp boyfriend saw in this was lost income, so to treat the lesions, he'd hold me down on the hotel bed and pour alcohol right onto those open sores. I would scream in pain, but he was unfazed.

The sleazy hotel where we flopped had twelve rooms sharing one toilet with a sink and shower, so cleaning up was impossible. But turning tricks depended to some degree on how I looked, so I'd go to a thrift store nearby, and behind the tall racks where they'd hang the pants, I'd undress and kick my dirty, pus-stained clothes under the rack, and dress in clothes I'd just stolen from the store. Then I'd head out to turn tricks.

Useless now even to a pimp

Finally, in a drug-driven altercation, the pimp beat me so badly he broke my cheekbone. The whites of both my eyes filled up with blood, and my black-and-blue eye sockets swelled shut. With a face like that, I was now literally good for nothing.

With a messed-up face and nowhere to go, I begged people to let me crash for a night on their motel room floor and desperately tried to turn tricks to hustle money to drink. People turned me down on both counts. Now I was not even good enough to sleep on the floor or get work as a prostitute. Could I get lower than this?

Living under a semi-trailer

Soon the streets were the only place left. In a parking lot next to a liquor store I knew well, a company had parked some semi-trailers. So I crawled under one of them and passed out on the ground.

I had found my next home.

During the day, I'd beg people coming to the store for alcohol; at night I'd hide myself as best I could from attackers who knew an easy prey when they saw it.

The liquor storeowner hated having me there. Sometimes I'd be drunk and unconscious; other times guys would climb under the semi-trailer and force sex with me, then fights would break out over who would be next. I peed in the alley. None of it was good for business. Finally the liquor storeowner decided he wouldn't sell alcohol to anyone buying it for me.

In the years ahead, I would find I could barely recall what had to have been one of the most hellish times of my life. I do remember the odd feeling of comfort from the buzzing sound of the streetlights as I lay on the pavement. And I remember waking from stupors feeling so pissed and thinking, "Oh, God. Do I have to do another day of this?"

Death didn't feel like an enemy; it began to feel like a friend who would relieve me from degradation beyond belief.

Gang rape

One afternoon as I slumped by the liquor store, four guys nearby drinking Mad Dog 20/20 noticed me.

"Hey, can you cook?" they yelled at me. "We are having a party today – can you cook up some potato salad and cole slaw?"

"I'm a really good cook!" I yelled back, trying to pull myself together. All I could think was, "Oh, God! I get to drink!"

So we started down the street together, one of the guys cocked his head toward an alley, and said, "Hey. I know a short cut." I didn't care where we were going, really, so long as the way led to alcohol.

But the short cut was a short cut to near-death for me. We ended up at the railroad tracks, and I realized too, too late a gang rape was ahead. They threw me the ground, and slashed open the soles of my feet so I wouldn't be able to run. One guy grabbed my head and began beating it into the rocky ground while the others took turns raping me.

When a couple of them realized I was probably going to survive the attack, they decided they would keep me. In the process of the attack, they had torn the zipper out of my jeans and ripped off my shirt; my shoes were gone. So the three of them walked me naked from the waist up, jeans with zipper torn out, bloody feet through blocks of neighborhoods to a house on the east side of I-70.

We walked passed people, but if I tried to cry out, my captors would punch me into silence. It was obvious I was the victim of a terrible wrong, but no one intervened. No one called police; no one tried to help.

Finally at the house, they locked me in an upstairs bedroom and for the next two days took turns beating and raping me. I was shaking uncontrollably. Yet oddly enough, in the middle of this nightmare, I remember thinking, "If these idiots would just give me drink, I think I could survive."

Sometime during the blur of the second day, I heard them downstairs trying to decide what they'd do with my body after they killed me. So, after the house was quiet and I figured they'd gone out, I pulled on a filthy long-underwear shirt left in the corner, and jumped from a second-story window. I was going to die if I stayed; what did I have to lose?

Survival?

I survived. Dazed and staggering I wandered to the City Market area and spent the night in an abandoned parking garage.

The next morning I walked through downtown Kansas City as city dwellers in their business suits came toward me, headed to their offices. As I came toward them in ripped out pants, a filthy shirt and bloodied bare feet, they parted like the Red Sea.

That night I slept in a place fewer than four miles from the home where I grew up, but I had moved a million miles away from that place and those people. My life had just barely been spared again, but for what?

Would there ever be a way back to that girl I used to be?

CHAPTER FIVE

HITTING BOTTOM

I should have died during the ugliness of the time under that semi-trailer; I surely wanted to. Instead, slowly I made my way off the street by doing whatever it took to attach myself to one awful man after another. The next couple of years passed in a blur of drinking, beatings, and rapes.

Until I found Herbie, the maintenance man.

When a drug-dealer boyfriend threatened to force me again into prostitution, I was terrified enough to ask for help from a scruffy, stumbling apartment maintenance man who was so glad to have a girlfriend he didn't ask questions. I didn't require hot love; I needed safety, and quick. Maybe this man could be my ticket out.

The predictability of life with Herbie opened the way for me to do nothing but drink. I no longer feared being beaten up, or dumped on the street. Herbie provided a roof over our heads, and he liked having me with him, chaos and all. And since he loved drinking as much as I did he kept us supplied in booze, so I wasn't pushed to do much of anything the next couple of years but drink.

And drink I did.

My drinking now moved into as much bingeing as my broken body would allow. I'd down all the alcohol I could until my Crohn's disease would flare badly enough to make me stop. But a week or so off alcohol would provide just enough recovery that I could start up again. Five times I was hospitalized, and at the hospital they'd always say, "You have to quit drinking or you are going to die." Now there was no murderous boyfriend to blame; I was taking my own life with alcohol poisoning, with absolutely no incentive to try to save myself.

The slow circle back to family

When I was working the streets, and running from rapists, and barely surviving under the semi-trailer, a sense of total worthlessness led me to completely cut myself off from my family. Now that my life showed the first semblances of regularity I'd had in years, I thought about reconnecting with my parents.

There were periods early in the binges when I thought I functioned well enough to pass myself off as almost sober. When I was sick between the binges, well…they knew I had Crohn's and had seen me sick before. So I cautiously reached out.

Connection to Dad?

While I had struggled to stay alive on the streets, my mom had moved into her own life-and-death struggle with ovarian cancer. My dad had been through a triple bypass, and was now facing back surgery as well. Now I was able to slip back into their lives as a helper, taking my dad to doctors' appointments, and occasionally doing things around the house for my mother.

During these nine months of edging back into each other's lives, we even had moments that looked vaguely like "family." To earn a little whiskey money, I had started making banana bread, cookies, and fudge to sell at a Saturday flea market. My dad, and sometimes my mom, would come with me to the market occasionally. For the first time in 34 years, I felt the stirrings of a connection to my dad. But that hope died with a phone call the day after we'd celebrated my dad's 61st birthday.

"Sissy," my mom yelled hysterically into the phone, "Get over here!" And without taking a breath, she blurted, "Your dad is dead."

My dad was dead.

I headed for the nearest liquor store for a bottle of whiskey. If there was ever a justifiable reason to drown my sorrows, this was it.

When I showed up at the house, my mom had only one concern: was Sissy going to embarrass her in front of all the friends who might now see what she had become?

She didn't say hello, or hug me, or look for comfort herself. "Sissy, please. There are going to be police officers coming through here; do not meet them reeking of alcohol. You'll disgrace your father's memory." Then she paused. "I'm going to call my doctor and get you something…" The "something" was 100 ten-milligram Valiums, enough to keep a fair-sized horse sedated.

Yellow taxi to survival

The mega doses of Valium got me through that week, in the middle of that drugged-out grief, I determined to quit drinking. "I'm finally going to make my daddy proud of me," I told myself. I scrounged some duct tape, stuck a piece around the quart of whiskey I had been carrying in my purse all week, then wrote the date on the tape. This date would mark my turning point, the last day I drank. Ever.

Only problem was, when I got home and ran out of Valium, I began to feel the gut-wrenching pain of having lost the man I searched for all my life. "I'll just have one drink…" I told myself, and popped the top and chugged whiskey until the bottle was empty.

When I came to sloggy consciousness after this binge, only one thing was clear. Getting sober was going to require help. In a decision that only those who know what "hitting bottom" really feels like, I called the only detox center I knew about and asked them to take me in. A yellow taxi with a driver who spoke no English came for me, and dropped me at a dark, bleak detox center downtown where I would take my first, stumbling steps toward life.

Detox to treatment

For the next week, I was one of 18 drunks holding down a bunk bed in the unfinished basement of an old building. I remember stone walls, two small windows with bars on them...and little else, except the sounds and stench of 17 other deathly sick men and women moaning and spewing vomit and diarrhea.

I fit right in. For 3-4 days I shook so hard I couldn't even hold a cup in my hand. They'd put a milk crate next to my bed with some food and Kool-aid, but I was wrenching so badly I couldn't hold anything down. My body was trying to eject 22 years of non-stop poisoning, and every part of me resisted letting it go.

I detoxed without dying and moved next door to begin a month of treatment.

For the next 30 days I went to 12-step meetings, and took classes on living skills, and brought snippets of my story to group therapy. None of this was revolutionary – I'd heard it years before when I went through treatment to avoid going to jail.

But then my dad was alive; now Dad was gone. I broke his heart in life; maybe in the wake of his death I could make up for my wrongs by finally getting clean and sober. I would become the daughter he would have wanted to come home to.

Life starts to change

Though my mother never said much about the decision to go to treatment, it must have moved something in her. She called one day with a surprise message. "Sissy," she said, "I know your dad would want you to be okay."

She went on. "I want you to start looking for a little house with two or three bedrooms. I will buy it, and you can get some clean, sober roommates to share expenses."

Was this my mother? The same woman who seemed to always find a way to shame and berate and blame me?

I had no idea what to think about her offer, but it occurred to me later that this might be her way to resolve guilt about ways she'd treated my dad. I found a little house in northeast Kansas City, near a support group with a 12-step program I was attending, and brought her the information. She wrote the check from my dad's life insurance money, and I had a home. When time came to move, I invited Ted, a guy I'd connected with through a 12-step program to move in with me.

A house of my own? This was a first. Maybe I really was starting a new life.

Finding purpose

Part of my recovery turned out to be storybook; I could have been a promo for a 12-step program.

First it was going to a daily meeting for myself, but soon their emphasis on giving to others took hold. At first, I helped because it made others like me, and I desperately needed to be liked. But then I started to understand helping others could make me useful in the world, and give me a reason to get out of bed.

I was still baking and selling goodies at flea markets; now I began taking what hadn't sold to the detox center where I'd been a patient. And with some of my flea market profits, I'd head for the tables selling hygiene stuff, and buy small tubes of hotel toothpaste and toothbrushes 10 for $1. I added these to my arsenal of gifts, and in the evenings I would sit on the beds of those miserable detox patients and along with the gifts, tell them my story. From there I started helping at the treatment center.

I'd never thought of myself as useful, except to desperate users with evil intentions. But inside the 12-step experience it was different. I was different. I found that when I served and gave, people I helped started changing for the better.

We'd even dance and party booze-free, and still have a great time! It was unheard-of in the world I'd come from, and it was wonderful.

Really? Church?

I was sober, and getting healthier, but not everything changed overnight.

My live-in boyfriend Ted started recovery with me, but eventually the call of the old life won out. At first when he'd relapse, I'd go to dope houses to try to find him and bring him back. But I soon found myself living out the same hell I'd inflicted on my family all those years. I got afraid to leave the house: what if he called for help and I wasn't there to answer? What if he needed me? But worse...what if he came home while I was gone and stole my stuff?

On one of these benders away from me, he went to a faith-affiliated place for help. When he came back, I found he'd actually started going to church. And, he thought I needed to go, too!

What? Church had never been part of my story, except for the few times when my brothers and I walked alone to a little church near our home. Well, those times and the time I went with a neighbor girl across the street to her Pentecostal church where I saw people flopping on the floor speaking in tongues. On the streets all I learned about faith was a mixed bag of confusion and weirdness. I would have said I believed in God, but I had no idea really what this religion stuff was about – and it looked like no place for me!

But Ted insisted. If I didn't go, we'd be something he called "unequally yoked" and well, he couldn't be with me.

In reality, I should have agreed we were unequally yoked. I was clean and sober – and he was a crackhead! But at the time I couldn't let him go, so I dressed up in my red miniskirt and headed out with him to get our praise on. Nothing took inside for me, but it kept us together, and that was all that mattered to me.

Rocky reconnection to Mom

Six months into my recovery, my mother's ovarian cancer returned and she desperately needed care. Because of our miserable relationship, I was afraid of relapse if I hung around her, but my brothers had families and demanding jobs. Besides, neither of them had hurt my parents the way I had; it was my time to do some repaying. I'd drive to her house every morning, take care of her all day, head for a 12-step meeting in the late afternoon, then go home to fix dinner and see how Ted was doing. The next day I'd do it all again.

One afternoon when I was holding a 12-step meeting at my house, I heard what turned out to be a police officer banging on my door.

"You Bobbi Jo Reed?" he asked. I cringed. If I was going to be arrested – and God knows there had been multiple things in the past for which I deserved arrest! – I seriously did not want it to happen in front of my support group. I stammered a little, and then finally said yes.

My mother had called them, he told me, because she needed to reach me urgently. As it turned out, her air conditioner wasn't working. Another time she made one of these emergency calls, I raced to her house to find she'd misplaced her remote control.

A lifetime of addictions to "legal" narcotics had left her in constant confusion. Because she was smoking while heavily drugged, I'd find burn marks all over the house. When I'd try to reduce the fire hazard by clearing some of the trash from the house, she'd wait until I left, then drag back inside whatever I'd put on the curb.

Most days, I left her house very frightened and deeply angry, and cried through most of the drive back to Missouri.

Finally, all alone

December 29, 1998 was a good day. I took Mom in for her regular doctor's appointment, and she looked more beautiful than she had in years. "Your insides must be made of cast iron," her doctor told her. "I can't believe how well you are doing." We went home relieved and a little giddy. I had a doctor's appointment the next morning, so called my brother and asked him to check on Mom since I wouldn't be there until later.

But when my brother went to her house, he found my mother in the living room, dead.

As I raced toward her house, I at first felt a flush of relief. For nearly my whole life, she'd been unhappy; now the suffering was done. And for most of my adult life, her ridicule and manipulation had defined our relationship; that, too was now over.

But relief was soon replaced with a deep wave of despair. So much had been wrong in my relationship with my mother, but now that she was gone, there was no hope anymore of making things right.

My brothers were sitting with Mom's body when I arrived, afraid to touch her. But I wasn't. I took the rollers out of her hair and got her more presentable for the EMTs – she would have insisted on it, I knew. Then I held her and kissed her as I said good-bye. The following day, December 30, I helped with arrangements, and bought the urn we'd use for Mom's remains. That night, however, I came home to a deserted house.

My mother had died, and at this time of deep pain, I had no one who cared enough about me to be there.

I'd felt lost like this before, but in those days, there was always something to numb the pain. Now nothing remained except the deep, wrenching sense of emptiness. I started crying – and praying. I had said The Lord's Prayer and the Serenity Prayer at Recovery meetings. But that night I knew they weren't enough. I'd had only three years of sobriety against twenty-two years of escaping into alcohol during times like this. The call of that old life was deafening.

I cried out to Jesus, "Lord, don't let me go back where I came from. And please, please show me where I am supposed to go and what I'm supposed to do...because I have never been so lost."

I fell asleep calling out to God more humbly than I ever had in my life.

CHAPTER SIX

RESURRECTION, AND A CALL

When I woke up on January 1, 1999 I really woke up for the first time.

The fear that had held me captive for nearly 38 years was gone.

In its place was a solid sense that I was going to be okay. All of life ahead of me was going to be okay. In place of the fear of not ever being good enough, not ever being loved, not ever being safe, I felt calm. Whatever had been so empty was now filled up. Bobbi Jo Reed felt comfortable in her own skin.

I had no idea how this inner transformation happened while I slept. But because of those few episodes of attending church, I had an idea of what had happened. God had heard me crying, and He came. His Spirit moved into the dark void that was my life, and filled me with His peace and deep, deep belonging to Someone who would never leave, and who would love me always.

Changes

What happens when God comes into your life? I didn't know. But I did know that with no conscious effort on my part, I started making different decisions, starting with my relationship to Ted.

On January 2 I got a call from a local hospital. Ted had been found passed out outside a liquor store the night before, nearly dead of frostbite, with an internal body temperature of 68 degrees. Did I want to see him?

The enormity of this change in me only makes sense if you know the story of the twenty-plus years before, and the parade of abusive men I'd chosen over and over and over.

When that call to see Ted came, I heard myself say, "No, I'm not coming. Not today. Not at all. He has others he can call, but he won't be living with me anymore."

Was this me? I felt firm, resolute. Not vengeful, or angry, or spiteful. Just filled with knowing that life with Ted was the wrong direction, and a new direction lay ahead.

Instead, my head began to fill with ideas for Mom's house. I knew we'd be inheriting it, and that it was nearly worthless in its present condition. I should move there, I thought to myself, and fix it up. This direction was as clear as the decision to break off ties to Ted. Though I didn't know it at the time, I was hearing God's direction for my life. It came so clear and simple – as it has repeatedly since – that it almost seemed obvious. This Savior who had come to live in me brought more than peace. He was bringing a purpose, a path, and potential to give. Whatever had happened inside when I called out to God was moving me toward a new way of life.

Starting a different rehab

Working on my mom's house gave a new focus.

The house was a long way from being a livable home for anyone. The years on too-many prescription pills had warped Mom's thinking in many ways, but one of the most obvious was in her relationship to Stuff.

Both the first floor and basement were packed full, in some places with only a narrow path between the shoulder-high piles. By the time I'd finished with the clean out, I'd filled four forty-yard dumpsters. Also, the way she had gone about hoarding kept me from being able to simply shovel everything out. Inside the pages of various magazines she'd tucked important documents, so each magazine had to be flipped through individually before it went to recycling, and everything inside every box had to be carefully checked.

Cleaning became the next challenge. She had four dogs who became incontinent as they aged, so the floors reeked of urine. All the carpets went immediately, of course, but it took three coats of polyurethane on both the top and bottom sides of the wood floors before the odor was sealed off.

The cleaning out and refurbishing took a year. I'd get up every morning and drive from my little house in Kansas City, Missouri to Kansas City, Kansas to clean or paint, or make decisions with the carpet layers or work with the plumbers as they installed new bathroom fixtures.

The rehab turned out beautifully. And it started a kind of rehab inside me, too. Though I was never consciously aware of this, while I stacked up piles of old magazines, God was stacking up piles of painful memories in me. And guilt. And anger. And sorrow for what I had hoped for in a home and hadn't experienced.

My heart was getting ready for a rehab.

Clean-up completed

Rehabbing the house took a year. When it was done, I put my little Missouri sobriety house on the market, and got ready to move into this re-created home.

My last night in that sobriety house, I wound up sleeping on a little palate on the floor because people were moving in the next day, so all my furniture was gone.

But I couldn't sleep.

I felt afraid to leave that house where I'd spent the longest sober period of my life since I was twelve. As I lay on the floor praying for God's help, a dark wave of emotion rolled over me. The bad things I'd done, the people I'd hurt, the lies and ugliness – and the pain of what had been done to me – it all came back at once in a flood of darkness, and I began to sob and I lay curled up on the floor beside my dog.

Suddenly, though I was alone in the house, I felt the sense of a strong, kind hand on my shoulder. A warm feeling started in my stomach and spread up to fill my chest.

There was no audible voice, but my heart heard these words: "You don't have to hold all this any more. You are forgiven. You can let it go."

There was another letting go that happened, too. I received God's peace about my parents' shortcomings. I could forgive them just as God had forgiven me.

From that time on, I felt a sense of peace between us. They had done the best they could with what they knew and who they were; now, with God's grace giving me what they couldn't, I could bless them and let go of anger and disappointment over failed expectations. There was no longer a need to blame them – or anyone else – for all that had happened in my past.

Later I would learn about "a peace that passes understanding." That describes the feeling that came to me as I left my little sobriety house for a different kind of clean-up.

Renewed house, new ways of operating

I moved to my mother's house the next day...or rather we moved the next day, if you counted my dog and cat.

Although my pets were good company, I never intended I'd live alone in this house. Ted the Crack Head had been left behind in Missouri, and after more than three years of sobriety, I looked forward to sharing life with a better Mr. Wonderful than I'd found on the streets.

But I was on a new track, even with the men in my life. Asking God's help seemed to be moving me in better directions than I'd gone in the past; maybe it would work with men, too.

I was aware that all those years in sick, abusive relationships left me with fear – and significant control issues. So, maybe besides someone who was clean and sober, it was time I considered a man who brought enough to the relationship that he didn't need a meal ticket, or a shelter-provider. In fact, maybe he should come with enough that he could pull half the weight of our life together.

I had no idea what this might look like, so I took a stab. "Lord," I prayed, "if you put another man in my life, give me someone who has his own place to live, his own vehicle, a job, and someone I can't control." I didn't want him controlling me; that was a drill I knew all too well. But I didn't want to control him, either.

Who came but an over-the-road trucker? He had his own vehicle, and inside that semi-cab, his own place to live. I couldn't control him because he was all over the country.

I got just what I asked for.

I got something else, too. My trucker boyfriend went to church, so I started going with him to the little fellowship he attended. In this community of believers, I learned more about the God who had claimed my heart. And I found accountability; the group was small enough that if I didn't show up, they'd know, and want to be sure I was okay. I began a new habit of weekly church attendance, a habit I found made sobriety easier.

Letting go of bad habits

At home one day I was walking down the hall, cussing at the dog, like I'd heard my mom do a thousand times. Suddenly in the heart of me, I heard a voice say, "You must have gotten out on the wrong side of the bed today. Maybe you should get back in that bed and try it again."

Again, no one else would have heard the voice, but I recognized it, and marched back to my bedroom, climbed into bed, then rolled to the other side and got out. As I stood up, I started to laugh. Really, I'd been getting out of bed on the wrong side my whole life. I laughed because of the truth of it, and because of the loving way this "you need a kinder attitude" message had come.

"This must be the way a loving dad corrects his kid," I thought to myself. Maybe I was being raised in this rehabbed house, but this time by a Parent with the strength and love to hold me to the best with grace.

Being helped gave a heart to help

The 12-step meetings put me in touch with lots of needs, and I was eager to give. When a friend had hip surgery, I jumped in to organize his care.

I'd signed up to clean for him, but I'd also committed to fetch a woman from jail who would stay with me for a short time. I took her with me to the injured man's house; by the time we left him she was acting more and more strangely.

I knew there was no alcohol in the man's house – I'd just cleaned it – so I couldn't figure out what was going on. She insisted she was fine, but I could hear the slurring in her words. "Breathe in my face!" I ordered. Minty breath. Turned out she'd drunk all three bottles of mouthwash in the man's bathroom. It was relapse, of course, so I let her know our next stop would be detox.

"Can I take a bath before I go?" she pleaded. She had been in jail, and the request seemed reasonable, so we stopped at my house to let her get cleaned up. But when she finished her shower, she walked into the living room wearing nothing but a towel and her purse over her shoulder, talking complete nonsense.

"Give me that purse," I ordered, and sure enough...non-aerosol pump hairspray. While in the bathroom, she'd drunk almost the whole bottle, plus a bottle of cologne. "You are getting dressed," I said, "and we are leaving right now!"

However, once in the car, she got in her purse to pull out a cigarette. As she lit it, I cringed. I knew what happened if you lit a match in a house filled with gas fumes; was she going to explode in my car?

We made it to detox safely, of course, but this episode would later serve as a warning that helping other alcohol and drug addicts wasn't going to be some hand-holding love fest. It would take gritty, gutsy, tenacious help to leave the old and choose the new.

Growing in giving

Some episodes of helping were dramatic, like my Jail-to-Detox friend, but most involved steadier giving, leading 12-step groups and working with many women who longed for a different way of life.

But they faced huge challenges. Most were victims of domestic violence or rape; many had had children taken away.

My heart would break as I'd see them leave treatment, and start with such great determination to find a new life. But most went back to old lives, or lives on the streets, or lives filled with abuse and rage and using. The deck was stacked against them.

When I finished treatment, I was given a fresh start in a safe home of my own. But most of these women in my 12-step group weren't so lucky. How would they recover when the people around them pushed them toward the old life? And how would they learn to be moms to their children without ever seeing what a loving home looked like?

Somewhere along the way I learned there were 900 women a year going through substance abuse detox and treatment, but only 30 safe beds available to them after they left inpatient treatment. Those numbers meant there was residential help for only 3% of the women.

What about the other 97%? Who would help them?

CHAPTER SEVEN

THE BIRTH OF HEALING HOUSE

An idea was growing inside me...

What if some of the women coming from treatment could come live with me? What if I could make a home for them where they could learn to live clean with the help of a loving family?

Interesting, I thought. But the obstacles were obvious. Though my house was rehabbed now, it had only 3 bedrooms, so I couldn't help many women. Plus, my neighborhood had rules against too many unrelated people living together, so though I already thought of these women as my sisters – or maybe my kids – the city regulations people wouldn't.

I did remember that in the downtown part of Kansas City, Missouri where I'd already lived in my little sobriety house, there were bigger houses. Of course the area wasn't exactly a Mecca of safety or tranquility. With drug dealers, gang members, prostitutes and their pimps, three hours rarely passed without the sound of gunshots. But in that tough neighborhood just off Independence Avenue they'd surely be more lenient when it came to community regulations. And houses were cheap.

So, I said a prayer for direction, and stuck a little notebook in the glove box of my car. For the next year or so, when I drove around my old neighborhood, I jotted down addresses of big houses that looked like they might work as a recovery house.

One place kept coming to my mind. Two blocks from the little house I used to own stood what I thought was an old nursing home. It was abandoned now, and up for sale for a year-and-a-half. I called the number on the realtor's sign repeatedly, but every time I'd get a message that the woman's voicemail box was full, so I couldn't let anyone know I was interested.

I kept looking.

Though I wasn't finding a house, my financial situation shifted. I'd invested my inheritance money from my parents' estate in the stock market. In 2002, the market tanked, so these investments tanked, too. By the time a $350,000 portfolio had dropped to $50,000 I decided to cut my losses and cash in the stocks; the broker helping me told me I'd have the money in seven working days.

So now I nearly had cash in hand. Did this mean it was time to buy?

After five days had passed, I arranged with a realtor to look at a big house just around the corner from that nursing home. It was beautiful, but I was out to help women, and the house wasn't arranged right for several to live there.

As I went back to my car, I said this prayer: "Lord, you know I'm impatient, and in a couple of days I'm going to have some cash. When You have found the house You want me to have, will You just drop it in my lap?"

A house in my lap

As I drove away from the house, and rounded the corner to St. John's Avenue, I spotted a realtor with people who looked like they might be buyers walking up the sidewalk to the abandoned nursing home. I pulled over, hopped out and ran up the steps to follow them.

"Can I see the place, too?" I asked.

"If these folks don't care, I don't care, either," the realtor said, so I joined the tour.

The house was awful. Streaks of mold grew on the walls. The place reeked of stale cigarette smoke and urine. Windows were knocked out; doors didn't lock, and at night homeless people camped in the basement.

Only a blind person would have seen potential.

Or maybe a woman on a mission.

There were 23 rooms, and the asking price was $50,000, exactly the amount I had coming in just two days. And because it had been a nursing home, it was zoned to allow multiple unrelated residents.

The house I needed had just been dropped in my lap; I informed the realtor I'd take it.

Homeowner

Now, I had a house. But what a house! Rats would think twice about living there in its present condition. Now, I needed money to make the place livable.

My only other resource was the family home I'd just spent three years cleaning out and making beautiful.

I'd never intended to sell that house, of course; I was going to settle down in this lovely home – and my clean-and-sober life – with a nice husband. Why else would I have installed a double Jacuzzi tub in the bathroom?

But God's provision of this 23-room monstrosity on St. John's Avenue was going to require I go all-in; no cozy backup life to escape to in Kansas. This recovery house would require me to sell my childhood home, and move back among the users I'd left three years before.

Making that decision wasn't hard because God seemed to be so clearly leading. Though the sale of my current house would pay for the rehab, I needed money right now to begin work. I headed for the bank to apply for a fix-up loan, and never looked back.

Installing the first lock

This house in which I'd just invested everything was sitting empty with broken windows and unlocked doors – and homeless people coming and going from the basement.

Didn't I need to secure it somehow?

I knew making that house secure was going to take weeks or months. So I called on the one security system I had come to trust. I went back to the house, and in a little closet just off the dining room near the center of the house, I put a 2x2-inch picture of Jesus. I told Him the house was His – so He would need to protect it, and make it a place where His love had free rein.

Adding street smarts

God was protecting the house, but I figured I ought to do my share, too. So, when I'd show up alone to begin cleaning, I thought about those homeless men in the basement. No one knew better than me the kind of threat they could pose. So when I entered the house, I'd stomp around as loudly as I could, yelling, "Come on, Bob! Hey, Bill. Bring in those buckets; we've got work to do." There was no one else, of course, but the noise and an image of a crew of big, strong men upstairs chased the squatters out the back.

I went to work with the fury of a woman with her hair on fire. After working on my mom's house, I was a master at hauling out junk, so it made sense to start there. I set up a Command Center in the basement, and jumped in to pull up the smelly, mildewed carpet. Two metal file cabinets had to be pushed aside to get all the carpet, but when I tried, they wouldn't budge. What could be inside?

I opened the first drawer; it was completely full of drugs. The second drawer, the second file cabinet – all were full of the same kinds of drugs. I could hardly believe my eyes. I couldn't imagine why the homeless people who had camped here hadn't discovered this stash.

All I could see in those drawers of pills was the Devil at work, trying to kill a work of God before it could even get started.

I filled up a 33-gallon garbage bag and on Trash Day hauled it out and threw it in the truck myself. No need to take a chance on anyone else stumbling onto this haul and making a different decision about it than I had.

Hauling out trash started the work, but soon I was banging down walls and putting up new drywall. A friend from the 12-step group came to help sometimes, but largely I worked alone. Putting in 16 to 18-hour days, I lost 60 pounds, fueled by energy driven by faith, something my friend Judi and I would later call "God Juice."

Every morning I'd pull on my sweats and get to the house as quickly as I could. Twenty-three rooms awaited recovery, and the women I wanted to help were waiting, too.

Misunderstood

That Christmas, I was more than a little scared to show up at the family dinner.

After nearly 7 years of sobriety, my brothers had gotten used to Bobbi Jo, the crazy alcoholic being clean and sober, and living a pretty normal-looking life in our parents' home.

Now I'm going to announce I'm selling the home I just beautified, cashing in all my investments-inheritance, and buying a 23-room abandoned nursing home in the hood.

I was sure they'd think I was using again.

They were as mystified as I expected. "Are you sure you are safe down there?" they wanted to know. "Is this really what you want?"

If my brothers were mystified, they weren't alone. When people I knew from the 12-step meetings heard about the house, they thought I'd lost it.

And some got mean.

One night when I was working alone in the house, two of the 12-step women barged in, and cornered me in a back bedroom. "We think this whole house thing is just a big con," they said accusingly. "You are going to use your influence in the recovery organization to try to make money for yourself. Bobbi Jo, you need to resign right now!"

I'd lived on the streets long enough to know the difference between fake-tough talk and real threats. I sucked in my gut, stood up straight and said, "Get the hell out of my house!"

My tough stance worked; they turned and left. But until then, I had harbored hopes that maybe my 12-step friends would understand the need the way I did for a safe place for women to recover, and help with this impossible task. That day, I knew I'd been wrong. It was me and God. If He didn't help, I had put all my money into a house no one would want in a place no one should live to do a work no untrained, unsupported person should try to do.

Going on

I moved into the house December 24, 2002, sleeping on a day bed in the living room.

On December 31, the first recovery woman joined me in the house. From then on, the requests didn't stop. While I continued to rehab the house, I'd save my money until I could buy another twin bed, and maybe a dresser at the thrift store so another woman could come to live with us.

It wasn't a mission; it wasn't a business. It was just Bobbi Jo's house. When I'd hear of homeless women coming out of treatment, I'd find them and say, "You can come and stay at my house." The recovery community I was part of spread the word, and soon 12 women lived with me in that pink house.

There were two rules: don't drink and drug; no boyfriends staying overnight. Otherwise, they were my sisters, my children. They lived with me as they recovered, while I worked to make a home for all of us. My calling, and my future had come to meet me.

Enter the Dope Man

Two months after I moved in, a Dope Man moved in next door.

Of course it wasn't like we'd had some happy suburbanites as neighbors before. We all kept a careful eye on the crazy lady who lived on the first floor of that house. She was always drunk, and far too-often waved around a machete knife. So we didn't initiate a lot of neighborly get-togethers.

But the Dope Man's move to the second floor upped the ante. He was easy to recognize; I knew all too well what selling drugs and running prostitutes looked like.

It didn't take him long to understand something different was happening next door to him. We weren't screaming or fighting, and men weren't coming in and out. And on Sundays, the little church I was attending would have praise services in my house, so the Dope Man and his girls got a heavy dose of God music once a week.

Once one of his girls ran to us for help, so the Dope Man got nervous about his business. To be sure we stayed away from his girls, he carried a pistol in the front of his pants and took to brandishing it when he'd see me or the women in my house.

The first time he pulled a gun on me, I called the police. But the Dope Man quickly ran back into his house, locked the door, and refused to answer when they knocked. The police left, and I was alone to deal with an armed, and now enraged, drug dealer. Next, he brought in female gang members from Chicago to intimidate us.

When fear would come pushing in, I thought about all the resistance I'd had to opening the house – the drug stash in those files downstairs, the criticism from my 12-step friends, now this drug dealer and his gang after us. It occurred to me that it wasn't the evil Dope Man we were fighting; it was a much greater Evil One who knew many lives were going to be saved through our house, and wanted to stop the work before it got started.

This realization gave me courage. Once I identified the Enemy I knew how to fight. I prayed for God's protection on our lives and on our house. If the work was God's, it was up to Him to keep it safe.

I saw changes immediately. Once one of the gang members confronted me, she pulled her arm back to smash me in the face. But before she actually threw the punch, her arm just dropped to her side, and she ran away. I hadn't threatened her; I hadn't moved; it was as though an unseen Protector stopped her. After that, none of us were ever so directly threatened again.

A year and a half later, the Dope Man started using his own product and moved out. We knew by then that God could keep us safe, but also that neighbors matter! So we began claiming the Dope Man's house for God.

Learning to guide recovery

While all this hoo-hah with the Dope Man was going on outside, inside my house we were learning lessons about being a family in recovery.

I wasn't trained in addictions treatment; I didn't have a master plan. But as I'd finish rehabbing another room in my new, enormous home, another woman just out of treatment would move in. And, since this was my home, and they were simply sharing it, I wanted them to find not just a drug and alcohol-free place, but a family who loved them; a family they mattered to.

Because they were my family, they quickly began to call me "Mom." And I just as quickly started making dinner for everyone at night. For women who had come from fractured homes like mine, and from abusive, lost years on the streets like mine, the idea of sitting down together to a meal their Mom had made for them was powerful stuff. It was love served up on a dinner plate.

I knew I couldn't support all 13 of us financially, so I borrowed ideas from another recovery house in town, and began to charge rent, plus some for food. And slowly I added some expectations about all of us keeping our rooms clean, and cleaning up after ourselves in the kitchen after we'd used it.

Thinking of us as a family made other rules easier to decide about, too. First, I knew recovery only works if you work it, so I required they had to be active in recovery – going to meetings, and having a sponsor. And I expected we'd all go to church to feed our spiritual growth, too.

Last, I started a weekly meeting on Sunday nights so we could talk things over – what wasn't working, and what needed adjusting. For a woman from a family that never talked about anything, this was a big step, but I knew firsthand the devastation that can come if issues aren't out in the open. It wasn't going to happen to this new family of mine.

And as I rehabbed their rooms, I worked hard to make them beautiful – pretty colors, coordinating window coverings and bedspreads, and pretty pictures on the walls. Now, most of this came from thrift stores, but I really shopped these stores, digging through the curtains to see which might work best with the other things I had, and arranging and rearranging pieces to make it as nice as I could.

It was freeing to know this attention to beauty wasn't about me; I'd had the chance already to remake my mother's home into a beautiful place. This was about giving others a place to live they were proud of, and where they felt, well...like princesses.

It never occurred to me to think of these women in my home as renters, or projects or clients. They were part of my family, women with hidden beauty that alcohol and drugs and abuse had stolen from them. We were going to find that beauty with God's help, and love it back!

Naming the house

Fortunately, because the Pink House had been zoned as a nursing home, I was already "legal" with the city to have unrelated people living there. Later I learned we should be incorporated, so one of my girls who had some business background helped fill out the application.

In the process of becoming official we had to have a name for the house. Someone suggested "Bobbi Jo's House," another "St. John House" since we were located on St. John Avenue. But neither of these felt right to me.

As I prayed about this, pictures came to mind of women who had been sent to me. They'd walked in with blank, dark, empty eyes, and soon God's love would become real, and that darkness would be replaced with the light of God's Spirit. Hope returned; life began to take root.

"It's healing," I thought. "This home is a place for healing."

So, Healing House it became.

CHAPTER EIGHT

FROM HEALING HOUSE TO HEALING HOUSES

The word was getting out about Healing House; we constantly had a wait list.

One day I got a call from a man I didn't know. He and his wife were part of the recovery community, he explained, and had heard about our work.

"Can you come to Perkins and meet my wife and me for dinner tonight?" he asked. "We have an idea for you."

As we finished our dinner, the wife said, "Bobbi Jo, two things I want you to know about us. We are not religious people; we don't go to church. And me and my husband have been married for forty years, but haven't slept together for 25."

I sat up a little straighter; I'm getting nervous. Where were they going with this?

"I'm telling you this," she said, "because a couple of nights ago my husband came in my bedroom at 3:00 in the morning and woke me up to tell me God had just told him we are to give you the money to buy the house next door to your Pink House."

"We are not crazy," the husband broke in, "but we can't explain this. Nothing like this ever happened to us before. We think we are supposed to help you get that house to help people in recovery. So, will you find out who owns it and what they want for it?"

Before that day, I had never thought of having more than one recovery house. Oh, I'd claimed the Dope Man's house as a place for God to be honored, but I thought His answer would come in the form of great neighbors. After this very unusual conversation, I felt I had to consider buying that purple house to expand our recovery mission. At least I had to ask...

Purple is the new pink

The house was for sale, with space where 12 women could live...for $37,000. That price should tell you two things: the desirability of our neighborhood, and the condition of the house. But this was our kind of house! It made sense that women re-creating their lives should recover in a house that was also re-created after being trashed from drugs and alcohol.

The couple who had offered to give the money to buy the house later reconsidered, and decided maybe God meant they should loan us the money instead. Either way, they were His instruments to get the ball rolling. With their loan, we made the purchase, and I headed to the bank to see if I'd qualify for another loan to repay them and to buy supplies for the rehab.

What do you know? The nursing home I bought for $50,000 was now valued at $194,000 – and I learned about something called "equity," a new concept to a girl who had at one point slept on the asphalt under a semi-trailer. With this magic equity from the Pink House, I was able to get a loan that would repay the couple that had helped us, and also added some to buy materials for the fix-up.

This time, an assist with the rehab came from men in another recovery house across town. When I paid them to help, they earned the money they owed to pay their share at the recovery house. Since our girls paid rent, I was delighted to help others in recovery do the same. The blessings from this purple house were starting to multiply, and we had yet to move in!

However, not every outcome of this expansion to two houses felt like a blessing.

A family of 24

With more women in our care, I had to get better organized.

I also had to get more deliberate about showing the girls what a mom's love meant. I would die for them, of course, but it also meant sometimes I wanted to kill them!

Like the time I was upstairs in my bedroom at the Pink House when I heard a loud bang coming from the direction of the auto repair shop across the street. When I looked out the window, I saw the auto repairman in front of the open hood of a car, engulfed in flames from the waist up!

I grabbed my phone and dialed 911.

Just then, one of the girls walked into my room. "Hold on," I yelled, "I'm on the phone...there's a man on fire outside!"

She didn't even glance toward the window. "God!" she muttered. "You never have a minute for me."

Did she not hear what I said? "There is a MAN ON FIRE outside! I'm calling 911!"

She groaned a little. "All I wanted to tell you was I'm going to get my nails done and go to Family Dollar..."

"Get out of my room." I said with more than a little edge in my voice. She was lucky no bodily injury went along with that order.

I understood where her odd response was coming from, but this was no time to provide counseling. We needed a fire truck!

Other episodes were less dramatic, but equally maddening. One afternoon I'd climbed two ladders to paint the eaves along the roofline of the Pink House, no small feat for a woman afraid of heights. As I'm painted, one of the girls came to the bottom of the ladder, yelling for me.

"Mom! Mom! You've got to come down right now!"

She sounded near hysteria, and in a family like ours, a crisis can be life-threatening, so I made my way, first down the ladder I was standing on, then across the roof to the second ladder that brought me to the ground.

"What's the problem?" I asked, a little out of breath.

"You need to hook up my VCR," she announced. "I want to watch a movie and the VCR isn't working right."

Seriously? This was her crisis? Again, God's grace in that moment protected her from a bucket of paint dumped on her head.

This disease of alcoholism is rife with selfishness, but my girls weren't the only selfish ones.

I had my own selfish nature to confront.

I've never been a morning person, so my ideal start to the day included (a) coffee, and (b) morning prayers, in that order.

However, as soon as I'd hit the kitchen, the girls seemed ready to pounce with issues, demands and emergencies. In my head I knew this wasn't intentional meanness; they were in the stage of recovery in which the world still revolved around them. But I began to feel like I was entering a room of vultures, waiting to pick me apart with their clamor for decisions and rescue.

Not only was I a failure in showing love, I could see burnout (counselors called it "compassion fatigue") looming ahead. Either my attitude or my routine was going to have to change.

With God's help, I changed both. First, I decided my prayer time would happen before my feet hit that floor, not later. Facing the day with a God-connection gave strength. And, maybe just as importantly, I moved a coffee maker upstairs, so I could meet my girls a little more awake.

However, this learning didn't take care of my feeling overwhelmed.

The help I gave had to be empowered by love, and too often my patience wore thin. I could see I needed a buddy to share the load and keep me on track in caring for this growing family.

Right-hand woman

God agreed I needed a helper, and chose Judi.

However, if you'd met Judi when she first came to us straight out of treatment, you'd have said she didn't appear to be a good choice to help anyone.

Her first admission to Healing House lasted about eight minutes. She'd just come from treatment, and was in such ill health she used a walker to get around. She was 56 at the time – I was 41, and still a tiny thing from the 60-pound weight loss when I was on the House Renovation Diet. The girls in the house at that time were all young. Judi took one look at me, then the others, and said, "I'm not moving in with all those skinny young girls!" and went drinking instead.

A few months later she came again, but this time her spirit was different. The treatment she'd just completed was her eleventh, and by age 56 she knew she wouldn't survive much longer in an alcohol-soaked life. So, this time, the day before she finished treatment, she prayed and told God, "If you keep me sober, I will serve you the rest of my life."

(Clearly she had no idea what she was saying. The next day she came to Healing House, expecting to stay three months. That was more than ten years ago, and she has yet to leave.)

By the time Judi joined us, my ability to fund us by myself had run out so I required everyone to pitch in on expenses and rent. Judi got a job cleaning house for a mean old lady. I could see that even though she dreaded going, every day she'd get on the bus and head to work. I respected her for it and took special care to do what I could to help her succeed.

Of course, everybody has a definition of "special care," and there were days Judi wished mine wasn't so special. As part of her recovery plan, on days she didn't work she was scheduled to attend outpatient treatment. But she resented it mightily. "I've been through treatment eleven times," she'd complain to me. "I could teach this class!"

I'd just push her toward the door, and when she'd step outside, I'd lock it behind her and yell, "Go to treatment!" She'd fuss, and make it clear she shouldn't have to listen to a young chick like me. But after a few episodes, she began to realize that even if I was younger, I knew how to stay clean and sober. Soon, we'd made peace.

It helped, of course, that Judi was growing spiritually, though the process wasn't easy. At first the Bible studies in our home would leave her frustrated. Because learning Scripture came hard for her, she'd often walk out of the study in tears. I'd find her crying upstairs, muttering, "I'm so stupid. I'll never get this." But she didn't give up, and in time she was running circles around me quoting the Bible.

Before long, I started asking for her assistance. I could see she had a kind way with the girls, and knew how to help around the house. Fairly quickly, she started helping more and more, and in time, it was clear she was taking the role of the right-hand woman I sought.

Our trust in each other continued to grow, and in the years that followed, Judi would become the true ministry partner and buddy I so badly needed. Healing House became her life as it had become mine. Everyone had always called me "Mom" but Judi would join me as "Mama Judi" and would consider these women, and later the men who came to us, her children like I did.

Sharing responsibility

Though the two Healing Houses were right next to each other, I could soon see I couldn't supervise life for both of them.

Because the Pink House was my home, I had 24/7 contact with the women there. Now that some of the women lived elsewhere, I worried about the attention and accountability they were receiving. The help had to be the same for all but there was only one of me.

What to look for in a house manager? The manager wouldn't have to carry the load I did. I'd be right next-door, and all of us would have dinner together at night, plus shared devotions and meetings in the Pink House living room. But she'd have to be a role model of sobriety, and willing to show love and discipline – a tough big sister to show the way, and help the women stay on track.

The house manager I needed actually came to me, bringing Starbucks coffee with her. Actually, I'd met our Coffee Friend during visits to the treatment center where I'd once been a patient, and we'd visit from time to time. When she heard what we were doing with the recovery house, she'd stop by occasionally to drop off coffee for us. I knew she was staying clean, and I liked the way she stuck to her commitments.

Could she be the manager I needed?

It was time to explore. When she'd stop with coffee, I began saying, "We've claimed the house next door to help more women. When God gives it to us, you are going to be the manager."

She thought I was kidding.

When we got the purple house, I made sure I was around when she stopped. "God just gave that house to us," I informed her. "I'll let you know when you need to move in." She'd shake her head and wave me off. But every time I saw her, I'd poke, "You packing yet?"

Sometimes it's hard to tell the difference between God's directing and a seriously persistent friend's nagging – but one of the two worked eventually, and my Coffee Friend moved in, then managed the house for two years. I would see later that this move to a house manager model would open the way for more growth, but at the time it appeared God was simply once again getting me out of a jam.

Strengthening for another expansion

By 2004, not yet two full years since I bought the Pink House, Healing House was now two houses, and bursting at the seams. We continued to make connections to referral agencies. Prisons, jails, judges, and caseworkers in Family Services – all were sending us people.

We were nearly 25 in number now, and between helping the girls with recovery, keeping up the business end of things, maintaining the houses, and cooking for everyone, I was again wearing down. But it took a call from one of my girls to help me share responsibility.

One of our girls had moved on, and was in her new apartment only a short time when I got a panicked call. "Mom!" she wailed. "Did you know hamburger cost $1.99 a pound?"

"I knew that," I said.

"Well, I didn't! And I don't have enough money to pay for my rent and buy the food I need!"

I felt ashamed. Cooking for everyone was my way to love and serve, but it was in reality a disservice. We needed to share the cooking and shopping load so everyone had a chance to learn.

So, a new practice emerged. Every night, one of the girls would shop for and make dinner for the whole family. To provide a meal for twenty-four sounded like a big expense, but since it was only happening every three weeks or so it gave opportunity to learn saving and budgeting and planning ahead. This change also helped increase a sense of ownership; this was everyone's family, not just mine.

Morning devotions became another group expectation. Each girl was to be out of bed, with room straightened up, and downstairs at the Pink House by 8:00 a.m. for devotions.

No one liked this idea when I instituted it. But I knew we needed to teach a life of discipline and order while we showed loving acceptance. Before we instituted devotions, I found one girl staying up most of the night playing online poker. But when the rule became up-and-ready by 8:00 a.m., the poker stopped. (You can't get up at 6:00 a.m. if you're going to bed at 4:00 a.m.) Plus, I knew starting the day with God's word and prayer would move us as quickly as anything toward recovery.

A place for new moms, and more

About this time, some of the girls stood out to me in a way they hadn't before. These were the pregnant women, who came to us because they were determined to stay clean for the sake of their unborn children. I was proud of them, so it tore at my heart when we'd have to send them out of our houses when they reached their eighth month. We had no facilities for newborns, no place these women could live with their babies after delivery.

I had to do something.

Half a block away from the Pink House, an apartment building stood abandoned. I'd periodically do what I called "window-peeking inspections" to see the condition of the place. During one of these episodes, a neighbor came over to ask what I was up to.

"I'm interested in this building," I told him.

He sent me to the owner of the thrift store down the street, who also owned the building. Fourteen one-bedroom apartments, I learned. However, the building had been vacant for several years and had dirt floors in the basement, so we'd be acquiring a sizeable rehab challenge.

With these apartments, I found myself learning new skills. For instance, that dirt floor in the basement had to be fixed, so with the help of Gary, a 12-step friend, we got a cement truck to pull up to the back of the building, and dump a whole load of cement down a chute stuck through the basement window. Gary and I waited at the bottom of the chute with shovels, ready to spread it out with some degree of evenness.

I laughed at myself while we shoveled that cement; construction training would have done me a lot more good than those cosmetology classes I took so long ago!

We started the interior rehab working from the top floor down, and as soon as we'd finish an apartment, a new mom would move in. In the spirit of the family we'd become, we decided to outfit the apartments with not just furniture, but also a crib, groceries, and baby things. Of course the furniture came from thrift stores, but it wasn't the labels or lack of scratches that made these places special. It was the sense that these children and their moms mattered to us, because they mattered to God.

Matching need to need

Not long after, another part of our family came to my attention. We were helping middle-aged women, many of whom started drinking after their husbands cheated on them, or after their children left home and they found themselves alone. Because they'd raised families, dorm life with a bunch of younger women was tough on them, but living alone was even tougher on their sobriety.

As I thought about their needs, it came to me we were missing a match made in heaven. The older women needed a more private living situation; the new moms needed guidance. Why not put them together in the apartment building? We began the moves, and found the win for both we'd hoped for. Parenting support helped the young ones; being useful helped the older ones.

The work seemed to have a rhythm now. We had several houses, and a sense of how to organize and lead them so women in recovery got support.

Now what? Requests continued to come; we always maintained a wait list. Should I look for more houses? Or was the ministry to go in another direction?

I listened for God's direction. These past four years "worked" because He had worked. Whatever was ahead had to be His work, too.

CHAPTER NINE

GOING DEEPER

2005. Instead of continued expansion, God decided to take us deeper and to strengthen the foundation He had laid.

We had lessons to learn about helping people recover with the emotional health and skills they needed to thrive. We would later decide that of the hundreds of lessons, four would be foundational to guide our future as a ministry.

Lesson #1: Being sober doesn't mean you're mature

The physical part of shaking an addiction isn't pretty.

I can tell you from experience it means vomiting, and diarrhea, and hallucinations...terrible stuff. There were times when I kept drinking because I was afraid of detox. At times when I'd try to stop on my own, I'd keep adding water to my "final" whiskey bottle because I couldn't live with the idea that it was completely gone. But when it was empty, I went to hell. I couldn't eat or drink; I couldn't talk to anyone I'd lay on the couch with a puke bowl beside me and hope to die before the experience killed me.

What I didn't know was this: the physical detox is the easy part. The emotional and spiritual renovations take more time, and sometimes more pain. We are now left to face all the problems we've spent a lifetime running from, but this time with nothing to numb the feelings.

Plus, when we start using, our emotional growth stops. I started drinking at age 12. So, on the streets, I was a 12-year-old girl in a 28-year-old body with no one who could stop me from ruining my life.

Women coming to Healing House were like me. They often looked like adults, but acted like defiant teenagers. It was as if they felt, "I've been sober a couple of weeks now; why isn't everyone in my life acting right? Isn't everything supposed to be problem-free now that I'm not drinking?"

Growing up in public is not pretty.

So when they'd think the world should revolve around them, I'd tell them stories. Like the time early in my recovery when I thought the people at my 12-step meetings were all slamming me. "They're having a good time; I walk in and they all shut up," I said to myself. "Must be saying bad stuff about me."

One night I decided enough was enough. "I've had it with all of you," I yelled at them. "I know you are talking about me. I am done!"

A guy at the table closest to where I stood looked at me a minute, and said, "Who in the hell are you?"

"Well, I'm Bobbi Jo Reed!" I answered. "You know me."

"No, we really don't," he said drily. "So why don't you sit down and shut up?"

Of course that made me furious and I stomped out. But I went back the next day, and this time I stayed with a glimmer of realization that maybe everything and everyone in the world did not revolve around me.

Like I said, growing up in public is not pretty. And we had a lot of it going on. Judi (she was Mama Judi to everyone now) and I both prayed for wisdom to know when to comfort and when to confront.

We'd have girls in the homes steal from us. I had treasured possessions I'd inherited from my mother stolen. And one very bold young woman used to sneak into my bedroom while I was asleep to get the key to the safe where we kept pain meds and cash.

This offered a chance for God to purify my heart about "stuff." Of course I'd be angry when someone I cared about would steal from me, but God consistently reminded me it was just "stuff." If I hardened my heart to help because of a few material things, I was off-base. I had stolen in the past; I'd done so much wrong. I needed to let go and forgive those who took advantage. Instead of carrying a vendetta against them, I needed to grow so later if they'd call at 3:00 a.m. asking to come home, I could practice Holy Amnesia, throw on my clothes, and go to pick them up without a moment's hesitation.

But also, we worked harder at helping takers become givers. We started taking up collections to buy supplies for homeless people, then went out together under the bridges where some of us used to live, not just to hand out food, but to pray with the people we found and tell them how we know life can be different.

We also looked for ways to teach serving that met the need created by addiction for instant gratification. Painting a wall, raking yards, sorting and hanging up clothes in our little clothing room. Becoming part of something bigger than ourselves had to be more than words – it took action.

Lesson #2: Recovery has to be chosen, not forced

Sometimes the work we were doing became heart wrenching, especially when a woman we'd invested our hearts in went back to her old life.

At first when people would relapse, I'd take responsibility for them. I'd pore over the AA Big Book looking for answers. What did I miss? What did I do wrong? Sometimes

I'd chase our wanderers to bars or dope houses to drag them back to treatment.

However, I quickly saw I couldn't force change. Though I hated to admit it, I was trying to dictate others' choices, something even God doesn't do. I had to realize none of us had a chance of changing until we were completely done with the old life. We choose recovery – and we choose God – when we are out of other choices. I had to stop protecting those I loved from hitting bottom so they could begin the journey upward to new life.

I also began to understand my pressure tactics had a self-centered twist. Sometimes under the guise of helping, I was actually trying to deliver myself from the pain of losing people I loved. So, besides learning to be willing to let others hit bottom, I had to agree to let my own heart break again and again.

Of course I was tempted to self-protection, to hold myself back and build walls so I wouldn't get hurt again. Then I remembered God kept His heart open to me for 22 years, until I was ready to come. The small sacrifices asked of me were nothing compared with redeeming love like this.

Lesson #3: Families of addicts need healing, too

Alcoholism doesn't just affect an individual; it can take down a whole family. I had seen this with my parents. In the worst of my years on the street when I was too ashamed to call my family, my dad would go to the morgue when he saw a police report listing a female Caucasian body. It was the only way he knew to find out if I was dead or alive. Only now that I have "kids" I love like my own do I understand what agony this must have been.

We saw lots of kinds of families. Some would drop off their son or daughter at Healing House, and made it clear they were finished with them. They'd had enough.

However, others held on too tightly.

They'd leave their child with us, praying for a turnaround. We'd go to work. Their child had to be up and ready for devotions by 8, and had chores to complete, plus recovery meetings to attend. Sometimes the kid would be on the phone to Mom and Dad with complaints. "This place is awful," we'd overhear. "We have to go to meetings. We have to pick...up...trash!"

Well, no grown child of theirs was going to pick up trash! They'd rush to the rescue and set him free, ignoring the fact that normal people in the world get up and go to work at jobs that aren't perfect, earning less than they deserve.

Recovery means taking responsibility, but sometimes parents wanted to protect their kids from the discomfort that being responsible requires.

Other parents stopped short of facilitating an escape, but did so much to "support" they slowed the process. Because they'd lived with disappointment so long to finally see a daughter sounding better, and looking healthier, they'd go around the rules and provide a cell phone or a car to get to work. But we believed that when things come too easily, you don't honor them. Work isn't a curse; it's a gift that has dignity attached to it. Struggling isn't evil; it's what makes us strong.

I felt for these parents, but I knew the other side far too well.

When I was using, I'd steal from my mom's purse, and pawn my dad's jewelry. I'd tell myself, "They have enough; I need this! How can I spend the weekend with my boyfriend if I don't take this stuff?" And on the way to the pawnshop, I'd think, "What's wrong with these people? If they'd just give me money, I wouldn't have to steal it!"

My parents weren't to blame for this odd rationalization; I was simply failing to take responsibility for my own choices.

Until I went into prostitution, my parents were my safety net. A boyfriend would throw me out, or beat me so badly I couldn't make it on my own, so I'd show up at their door and move back into my old room. No one asked questions or said a word; no one said anything. I'd just stay until I was better or found another love, then I'd be gone again.

Through my childhood, I deserved better than I received from my parents, but they deserved better from me, too. I abused them as much as they abused me, but we were caught in a downward spiral we couldn't break. We desperately needed help, not just for me, but also for all of us. So it was easy for me to feel compassion for these suffering parents. Some we could help; others we couldn't.

But one message we consistently delivered: you can't help your child unless the child wants help. The best program, the top-of-the-line treatment center – none of these work until the addict says, "I'm at bottom. I have to change."

But we had hope, too, from seeing turnarounds.

After my friend Judi's life began to change, her family changed, too. During her years of moving from treatment to treatment, her children had given up on her in shame and despair. But as she got healthier spiritually and emotionally, her children slowly began to grow in trust, and to respond to her love for them. In time they began to call her for advice, and complain they didn't see her enough.

Stories like hers strengthened our faith. If we all stayed at this business of recovery, healing could come not just to individuals, but to families, too.

Lesson #4: Laughter is a powerful healer

Normal families have fun together, but few of us came from normal families. So we learned we had to get intentional about fun. The Healing House tribe started at recovery dances around the area – and we'd be the ones out in the middle, acting the goofiest.

We began to celebrate holidays, and not just the "big" ones like Christmas, Easter and the Fourth of July. New Year's, Valentine's Day, St. Patrick's Day…pick a month and we could likely find a holiday to celebrate with barbeque and movies and music.

Besides the new dimension these added to our family life, these celebrations also helped me recall some of the things I could appreciate about my mother. She loved to celebrate holidays with pretty decorations and great food. As I began to grow in new ways to show love to my family, I could now also see ways my mother showed love to us, even though she struggled so deeply.

Growing up, our family took camping trips. Now with my Healing House family, I started camping trips, and stayed alert for ways to make these unforgettable.

Like the time Judi and I ran across some silly men's boxer shorts with plastic tushies attached to the rear end. Too good to pass up! We bought two pair, and each put them on under our sweat pants and long shirts.

That night at the campfire, we took over the cooking, and as we bent over the fire to stir the soup, we pulled the back of those sweatpants down just far enough, and made sure we really bent over the fire, purposely exposing what looked like our bare behinds.

The kids were stunned. And just like you wouldn't know what to say if your mom's behind was inadvertently exposed to all your friends, they sat silent. Their shock and embarrassment started us laughing so hard we could barely stand up to tell them the truth.

I realized then that laughter was beginning to fill our life together so completely it was becoming our new normal, and that seemed to me like progress.

Besides the goofiness, we found having pets in the houses helped accelerate healing, too. Besides making life feel more like than "home" than an institution, these dogs and cats contributed in ways I hadn't expected. It seemed like the animals sometimes knew before we did when someone's heart was hurting. A couple of times when my dog disappeared, I found her in a girl's room room, curled up quietly next to someone in need.

Now, with more strength, growth lay ahead

During our first four years or so as an addictions recovery ministry, God directed us to build an infrastructure of love – welcoming houses, order, expectations, a start at faith…

In the four years that followed, I could see He had taken us deeper, strengthening us to help with more wisdom, and a better mix of tenderness and toughness.

Now, though we couldn't see it coming, He was about to shift our focus from going deeper to *going wider*.

CHAPTER TEN

GOING WIDER

With a family now of 60 or so to support, money was a continual issue. Some of our folks were getting help through a program started under the Bush administration that gave small grants to folks in recovery. However, these grants plus some rent payments barely covered our basic needs. We had a few donations coming in from people who wanted to help, but I continually looked for ways to make money.

In one of these ventures, I worked at a designer clothing sale in De Soto, Kansas. When the sale was done, I'd also leave with clothing donations we needed desperately. (When women came to our houses, they usually brought only a plastic grocery bag with all their belongings. Life on the streets doesn't include clothes closets or matched sets of luggage.)

At one of these sales I met a man who had a company called "We Buy Ugly Houses." He came to the sale as a driver for his wife, and we began to talk while she shopped. I told him about the ministry; he asked for my card. That was that.

A year and a half later, I was flat on my back with pneumonia when I got an unexpected phone call from the "ugly houses" man.

"Bobbi Jo," he started, "I came into work today and your business card was plunked right in the middle of my desk, right where I put my laptop."

"Hmmph," I responded. "Did your secretary dig it out for you?"

"No," he said, "and that's why I'm calling you. I can't figure out how this happened, but your business card got out of my Rolodex and onto the middle of my desk today. I figured it had to be God telling me to call you."

"What do you think He has in mind?" I asked, since I didn't have a clue.

"I have a house somewhere down there by you," he said, "and I'd like you to check it out...see what you think."

"I don't have any money," I said quickly.

"Everything I've tried to do with it has fallen through, and you keep coming to mind. If you can use it for your ministry," he told me, "I'd be willing to give it to you. "

Free house? Pneumonia or not, I felt instantly better!

The house was in awful condition, but it had another handicap. All our houses were on rough streets; I was used to gunfire and pimps. But this area was worse. A bunch of tough-looking men sat out in front of the house, drinking, then throwing the beer bottles at another abandoned apartment building across the street. Drunken men gathered in front of two other houses close by.

I could never bring women into a situation that risky. We'd be asking for trouble.

However, even though women wouldn't be safe there, men would.

The move to begin helping men

People had suggested at different times we expand the ministry to help men, but I always resisted. I figured I had already helped too many men in my life…way too many!

This time, though, the idea seemed God-instigated. The fact that He made this house free caught my attention, made me consider the option differently. I accepted this generous offer; we went to work stripping off five layers of wallpaper and turning the house into a real home.

(I was told I'd need some fancy chemicals to remove all that wallpaper, but they didn't seem to work. So, I tried vinegar. Worked like a charm, though to this day the house smells a little like a big Caesar salad.)

A second men's house

As I worked on that rehab, and thought more about safety issues, my mind went back to our early days in the Pink House. When we were the only ministry outpost on that dangerous street, I felt very vulnerable. Though we trusted God to protect us, the girls bought me binoculars for Mother's Day, and I watched the streets like a hawk from my second-floor bedroom window.

But when we took over the Dope Man's house next door, I felt safer. We had established a stronghold now. Jesus sent His disciples out in twos; the Bible said, "Where two or three are gathered in My name, I am in the midst of them…" Maybe there was something about this "going-in-twos" idea that went beyond St. John Avenue.

Next to the new men's house, there was another abandoned house. I didn't know much about real estate, but asked enough people to find my way to the tax records that told us it was owned by a holding company in Florida. Of course we called.

"Lady," the owner said, "I sell 100 houses at a time; I can't be bothered with just one home." We explained about the ministry, so he said, "Shoot me a bid. If you hear from me, you've got it; if you don't hear, don't call me back again."

We sent a bid and didn't hear back.

A month later I asked Judi to call him back; this time he was less welcoming. "Lady," he barked, "Didn't I tell you not to bother me again?" The door looked closed.

But I couldn't get the house out of my mind, so six months later I checked the tax records; he was still the owner. So I prayed, and dialed his number. When I heard that gruff voice answer, I said, "Sir, I know you told us not to call you again. But I've been praying about this, and I know without a shadow of a doubt this house is to be used for our ministry."

What else could I say? It was true.

At that moment, I believe God simply softened his heart because the voice that responded wasn't as harsh as before. "Well," he said, "if you've been praying about it, there must be something to it. Shoot me another bid."

We got the house.

In the process of rehabbing it, I was outside planting some flowers when a neighborhood woman stopped. "I want to tell you how grateful we are you have come to this part of the neighborhood," she told me. "Now we feel safe walking to the bus stop. And if our kids are in trouble, we know your people will help."

Before this comment, I would have said we had just been called to change lives. Maybe we were also being called to help change a community.

Learning to help men

Having men in the ministry called for adjustments on eve-ryone's part. They joined the family dinners right away, so all of sudden we had a hormonal component to our get-togethers that hadn't been there before. Some of our girls tried to mother them; others tried to attract them. I had a new package of challenges to trust God for!

So, a few new rules about relationships came to be. No pairing up. "Two dings don't make a dong," I'd tell the fam-ily, "and two sick people don't make a healthy person."

Mostly I pushed the idea that this was a once-in-a-lifetime opportunity for all of us to experience true brother/sister rela-tionships in a safe place. Most of us only knew odd, dysfunctional, using-based relationships with the other sex; this time it could be different.

I also had some things to learn about helping men become disciples of Jesus. It was soon clear we'd need the help of other men to accomplish this, and in time we partnered with a men's group from a suburban church for Bible studies and men's recovery groups.

At first the men who came were desperately needy, much more even than the women I'd started with. But as some be-gan to grow, they set a strong pace for the others coming in, and in time the family felt less like a sorority and more like a true family.

Beginning to add new services

Now with the growing numbers of people we were help-ing, our slap-dash business organization was finally catching up with us. Between admissions and caring for the "kids" God had brought to us, we had bills to pay and books to keep. Some were donating to the ministry now – we'd taken on of-ficial "non-profit" status, so there were receipts and tax forms to keep current.

Mama Judi and I were not sure we were paying enough at-tention to what mattered most: the men and women who had been entrusted to us.

So, we took a big step, and hired a couple of office staff. But now we needed a place for them since working out of their bedrooms like Mama Judi and I had done wasn't feasible anymore.

A drug crowd who lived two houses down from the Purple House finally left the area. It occurred to me their house could become a different kind of addition to the ministry.

This little house would work well as an office – the loca-tion and size were right. And it had a basement. I'd already been thinking about how we could help our folks with educa-tion needs. Some were working on GED's and learning to write resumes. If we had a little education center, we could teach them skills and do more to move them into the workforce faster.

We bought the house for $27,000. When I announced the purchase to Mama Judi, she looked pleased. "We have $2,000 in the bank," she assured me, "and I'm pretty sure we can borrow the other $700 somewhere."

Her face dropped when I made it clear the price was 27 thousand, not 27 hundred.

"Where will we come up with $25,000?" she choked. "You didn't sign anything, did you?"

Of course I had, and got on the phone to people who'd said they'd like to help us. The money came to God's glory and Judi's relief.

Also, the Kemper Foundation in Kansas City helped by paying to remodel the basement and to install computers so some retired teachers who had offered their time had a place to teach those ready to learn.

Later, Kemper would help us again when we saw the need for a Day Care to help mothers in recovery who couldn't afford to pay for good care on the starting wages they were earning. We had bought a little house in the area that would allow for childcare on the first floor, and space for the childcare director to live upstairs.

Services continued to expand, a step at a time. How far we could go I had no idea, but for now, God was leading and providing, one project at a time. Our job was to trust and follow.

New partners support the expansion

Occasionally I'd get invitations to tell the story of how God saved me, and how He was now saving others like me through Healing House.

One of these invitations came from a recovery-oriented group at the United Methodist Church of the Resurrection, a large church in the suburbs. After that event, something strange and wonderful began to happen. People from the church would call me to ask how they could be praying for the ministry; others wanted to know if there were ways they could help.

All my "kids" had gone to church since we started the ministry; I couldn't imagine how recovery would ever work unless something happened to connect them to God. On Sundays we'd load up into cars and drive to a little church where I'd attended for worship. We found ways to help there, too, in service projects and volunteering to cook for church gatherings.

This time, these church people were calling to see how they could help us.

I wasn't sure what to make of it. Though people had given us financial help from time to time, we'd never seen ourselves as a charity, really. We were more a family who helped each other to live healthy and clean lives.

I decided we'd test the waters, so I asked our new church friends to just come work alongside us.

For instance, when we did our Spring Clean-up Day, I told a bunch of willing suburbanite women to bring their rakes and come join us. This early attempt had a mixed outcome; working together gave a great chance for my kids and these volunteers to establish awkward connections. The event came to a surprise ending, however, when one of the rakers stirred up a couple of snakes in the yard. The yard emptied as screaming women ran everywhere.

Our new friends proved to be resilient, however. We decided that since we were the body of Christ and He was bringing us together, there should be more ways we could help each other.

In time, church members helped rehab new residences. Then a music group showed up to provide praise and worship for our Friday night community meeting. Soon, Tom Langhofer, a leader in the men's ministry and a recovering alcoholic himself, heard God's call to start a weekly Alpha class for us, teaching the basics of the Christian life. He recruited his suburban friends to serve as small group leaders, so more friendships continued to form.

Another minister, Dr. Pam Morrison, who had worked in prison ministry and addictions, understood quickly how pastoral counseling could add a deeper dimension to the services we provided, and began working with us.

In the midst of these new relationships, Colonial Presbyterian Church, another south Kansas City congregation, invited me to attend their women's retreat and speak about the ministry. From that beginning, we quickly came to appreciate each other, and they took the lead in making our girls a regular part of their women's retreats, and then coming to our homes to lead a weekly Bible study. They later offered to share their Soul Healing ministry, making times for individual prayer sessions with our family members who had suffered trauma or abuse.

Receiving and giving

These brothers and sisters from the suburbs were giving so much; we needed to give back.

I was delighted when the leaders of one of the church's annual blood drive asked if we'd like to staff a phone bank, reminding people to donate blood. And soon after, an organizer for a large annual conference the church hosted asked if we'd help with the event, stuffing packets, running errands, or whatever was needed.

Also, the churches helped supply us with backpacks we could deliver to the homeless on Christmas and Easter. They'd be filled with food, personal care items, pen and paper and a New Testament. Each contained a letter, telling them God had chosen them for a gift today because they were precious to Him. We'd be sure to ask each recipient's name when we gave the gift, and also ask if they'd like us to pray with them. Each who was willing received a hug along with the backpack.

Events like this gave us chances to serve, but more importantly, to serve right alongside people who wouldn't have personally known addicts or street people. We all learned how much alike we were in God's family, and the trust building went both ways.

Next, a vision for families

A man named Ed Schulteis heard me speak at a recovery meeting, and knew at once God was calling him to help us. Ed had a background in mortgage lending, so had real estate on the brain.

As we got to know each other, he heard me talking about my heart for families. We were helping singles, new moms and men. But as our people got healthier, those who had lost their children to the foster system were getting them back. Since our one-person apartments couldn't accommodate them (the child protection system has strict guidelines about the number of rooms that must be provided, etc.), these parents would have to leave Healing House.

But I believed they were leaving at just the wrong time. Because most of our people had low-wage jobs, the housing they could afford too often came with dysfunction, despair, and people in addictions. It's hard to stay sober with a drug dealer one floor down, or when the people across the hall are throwing drunken parties.

If we had two-bedroom apartments as part of the ministry, we could help support these newly restored families. There'd be safety and accountability, and a chance for the kids to get to know adults who were clean and sober.

Ed took this as a personal challenge. "I want you to look at this apartment building over on Independence Avenue," he told me excitedly.

"We're not going there," I told him. Independence was still notorious as a "strip" where crime and prostitution flourished. "We're rebuilding a safe community on St. John Avenue," I insisted. "We need to stay right here."

Ed couldn't hear the word "no," so I went to look. The place was beautiful; newly remodeled, with hardwood floors; it had two-bedroom apartments that could be converted to three-bedrooms if we needed.

But that's where the beauty stopped. Half of the 12 apartments were rented to veterans, many in addictions. We'd have to take the chance on filling half the apartments while we worked to vacate those who weren't drug-free. Plus, I couldn't get a loan and the owner refused to carry the loan for us.

I thought the door was solidly closed until the day the building owner called me, and asked to meet me at the Pink House. "My wife and I have decided we'd like to carry the loan for you," he told me. I was surprised, and amazed. As we began talking details, I suggested we move to the living room where it was more comfortable.

As he rounded the corner from the kitchen, there sitting on the sofa was a granddaughter the family hadn't seen for three years! She'd been in an abusive marriage, and she'd disappeared. The family didn't know if she was dead or alive.

Now, here she was, safe and growing in a recovery program her grandparents had just chosen to help – before they knew how God was already using Healing House to restore their family.

If any of us had had questions about whether or not God was leading us to expand the ministry in these new apartments, our answer was sitting right on that sofa.

CHAPTER ELEVEN

GOING FORWARD

Even though our family continued to grow, we kept up our practice of having supper together every night. It's what a family does, I thought. But we could no longer fit in the Pink House; the family needed room, something bigger than any of the houses could provide.

The answer came quickly. A couple of weeks later, a realtor's sign went up in front of a grocery store down the street; we were able to rent the storefront, upstairs and basement for $900 a month. After painting and a fix-up, this hall became our family dining room, plus a meeting place for all kinds of recovery activities.

What God provides, He protects

Our hall made up only part of a larger building; the space on the other side of our east wall was used as a mosque. I often thought how funny this was, that on a street as rough as St. John Avenue, not one but two faith groups would have a presence, and even share a building.

One night when I was letting the dogs out, I looked down the street from the Pink House, and saw orange in the sky. The hall was on fire! I ran back in and called the fire department. By the time we rounded up our folks, the street had been barricaded, so we made a prayer circle and claimed God's protection, and prayed the materials and equipment we had stored in the basement would be okay.

As it turned out, the fire started in the area inhabited by the mosque, so that part of the building was completely ruined. So much water had been poured on the building, we were sure our stuff would be ruined, too.

But when we were able to get in to inspect, nothing in our hall had been touched; there was no damage from water or smoke. No one had been hurt in the fire, and our Muslim neighbors were able to relocate to a nicer building in the neighborhood.

When the debris was hauled away, there on the exterior wall on the east side of our hall, in the design of the brick that had previously been covered up, was a six-foot high cross.

Seeing that cross looking out over our neighborhood is a message to me of what's happening as God comes to St. John Avenue. We don't hear regular gunfire anymore; there are no longer drug dealers and prostitutes on every corner. Instead, you'll find moms walking on the street with kids in strollers, and people picking up trash, instead of making trash. A place of fear has become a safer community.

God is good in the hood

What started as a recovered nursing home has become a mission providing homes and help for about 110 adults and 25 children. Over 2,500 people have come through our program.

Numbers tell part of the story, of course, but it's the people stories that fill me with praise.

Like the Christmas Day when we had filled up the van with our kids, and headed out to give backpacks to homeless folks. We'd stopped briefly at a Quik Trip to use the bathroom and get coffee. When I came out of the store, my heart stopped.

Next to the van with six of my girls inside was a police squad car. Since I knew all six of the women in the van were former prostitutes, I winced. Did some of the girls still have warrants out for their arrest? How much bail bond money was this going to cost, I wondered.

"Mom!" One of the girls yelled at me. "He's calling for back-up!"

Worse than I thought! Had the girls resisted?

Then the larger of the two police officers approached me...and gave me a huge hug!

"This is amazing," he said. "We know these girls, of course, and because we haven't seen them on the streets, we thought they were all dead. But we haven't seen them because they've turned their lives around!"

"Lady," he said, shaking his head, "You've restored my faith today."

Just then the back-up squad car arrived. But we discovered the additional police officers hadn't been called to handle a rough situation. They'd been called to come witness a transformation of lives.

From recovery to work

Now we are growing a deeper vision. Men and women get clean here, and get a strong spiritual footing. But we need to keep helping them to learn to live healthy lives.

They need training for work and help getting better jobs. (Try putting on a resume that your previous work experience involved dealing drugs or time in prison. This does not send you to the top of the "desirable" pile.)

Also, to get better jobs, they need skills like basic math to figure out how to measure carpet for a room or correctly split the check for a group's lunch order.

So, when the hall we were renting came up for sale, I began to see how we might help. If we owned the hall, we could install a commercial kitchen, and use it to open a little café (I imagined training for sous chefs, short-order cooks and wait staff), and a catering service (I could see training event planners and banquet servers). In another space, we could open our own thrift store, both to provide clothes for the people in our program, and also to train them in retail sales skills.

Asking price for the hall was $175,000. We could put $50,000 down, and the owner agreed to a balloon payment of $45,000. With God's grace and help, a silent auction for Healing House that the year before brought in just $12,000, this year raised $48,000. Plus, the money came just in time to make that balloon payment! We are well on our way to paying for the hall.

Now the hall needs to be completely renovated to make the dream of this vocational training come true, but the God who has provided all along will provide once again, in His way and time.

God is giving other dreams

Inpatient treatment centers are becoming a thing of the past. They're costly, and often serve people who don't have resources to pay. But I know from experience how critical those first thirty days of sobriety can be to beginning a new life.

When rockets go into space, most of their stored fuel is spent getting from the ground to the edge of our atmosphere. After that, the sailing gets smoother.

It's the same with recovery. Those first days of moving from addiction to sobriety take enormous effort; I want as many as possible to have the support they need to escape the "atmosphere" of addiction and come join us in recovery.

So, a part of my dream for the future is the addition of a treatment center, so those beginning this journey can start with all the help they need in the community of Healing House brothers and sisters who will care for them.

And I want a home specifically for pregnant women in recovery, so they can spend the months before their child's birth preparing not just to make a clean life for themselves, but for their babies, too.

There are many to help, but the God who helped me and now thousands of others through this work will find a way to help these, too.

Lost and found

A couple of years ago I was leaving one of the apartments after putting finishing touches on a place for a new mom to bring her baby home from the hospital. Suddenly, in the parking lot, a flash of remembrance came to me.

From all those years ago, when I was at my lowest, I remember walking by a man living under a highway underpass. Under that bridge he had a loveseat, a lantern and a mattress.

A loveseat, a lantern and a mattress.

I remember a feeling of envy – and longing – welling up in me. *"If I could just have what he has,"* I thought to myself, *"I'd have it made…"*

Now I was leaving a building with fourteen apartments to go to one of many beautifully furnished homes where I shared life with brothers and sisters who, like me, had given up hope but found it again as God found us.

In that parking lot, I began to cry.

God recovers. He redeems. He restores. He finds the lost and brings them home.

I know because He found me, and now graciously allows me to help with finding others who as lost as me.

A message to addicts, and those who love them

You know my story. You know few have come from a darker place, or come to a place of richer hope.

If you struggle with addictions, or you love someone who struggles, I have three thoughts I'd like you to take with you.

First, don't let shame or fear stand between you and a new life.

Most families in the United States include someone with an addiction issue. But the stigma against admitting it is so great that we work hard to hide the problem. Sometimes parents and family members pretend there's no issue because they fear they might be to blame.

Hiding and denying don't solve anything; they only stand in the way of getting help.

The truth will set you free though it won't make you instantly pain-free. You'll find though, as I did, that facing the truth, then gaining courage to face the pain will break down those walls that imprison you. It happened for me; it can happen for you.

Second, your first focus of forgiveness needs to be yourself.

We both know the drill. Get in trouble and shoot up a 911 prayer for deliverance, then forget all about it when things improve. You've done this dozens of times; so have I. Because we know ourselves, we don't feel worthy of forgiveness, or of anyone's love

But Jesus came for people just like us – the broken ones, the prostitutes, the cheaters, the liars, the sinners of all kinds. If you don't believe me, dive into His story in the Bible. As He met these, He forgave their wrongs, and called them to follow Him. He wants to wipe us clean.

Let Him. Accept His forgiveness, and then forgive yourself. Set yourself as free as He has.

Third, let your pain become your passion, and your mess become your message.

You've seen how in my life that the qualifications for the work I do came from the messes of the first half of my life. I love addicts because I am an addict. The very misery that nearly destroyed me has now given me a message. The same will happen for you.

I am living proof of God's unmitigated power to save and transform. If new life, freedom, belonging, and usefulness could come to me, these are possible for anyone who trusts Him. Recovery takes time; this isn't an instantaneous process, but it is waiting for anyone who will come.

May I close with a promise?

It's a promise that both keeps me alive and living to the full every day, because it's a promise from Jesus Christ Himself. He described Himself and His work this way:

The Spirit of the Lord is upon Me,
for He has anointed Me to bring Good News to the poor.
He has sent me to proclaim that captives will be released,
that the blind will see,
that the oppressed will be set free,
and that the time of the Lord's favor has come.

Luke 4:18-19 NLT

I know for myself that He brings Good News, and release, and sight and freedom because He has done all these things for me.

May His healing and release and freedom grow in you, too, as we let His favor rest on us in all the days ahead.

ACKNOWLEDGMENTS

I am eternally grateful for God, who gave me new life, then blessed me with not just the home I longed for, but also many homes to share with others.

Thanks to my dearest friend and ministry partner, Judi Burkholder. You make life and ministry a joy.

Thanks to my family, Greg and Dana, Jeff and Tammy, and my nieces and nephews for your love on the journey.

Thanks to the leaders of the Healing House team, especially Rhonda Thomas, Bob Dizmang, Jim Riley, Gary Babbitt, and so many others.

Thanks to the volunteers and partners who help build spiritual strength into recovery:
- Tom Langhofer and the Alpha Team
- Ed Schulteis
- Colleen Aegerter
- Pastor Mary Brown and the Soul Healing Ministry Team
- The Colonial Presbyterian Monday Night Bible Study leaders
- Dr. Rev. Pam Morrison
- Rev. Adam Hamilton, Rev. Jim West, Rev. Scott Chrostek, Rev. Todd Mayberry, Rev. Jeff Kirby, and Randall Leonard who have made us part of their church families.

Thanks to the volunteers and partners who pound and paint and pour and persevere to make the homes of Healing House so beautiful, with special thanks to:

- Rod Bosma
- Bob Svoboda
- Chuck Howard
- The Thursday COR Construction Team

Thanks to Allen and Madeline Tollefson, Daryl Rodrock of Rodrock Development, and the Kemper Foundation for generous support.

A special thanks to Marilee and Joe Benage, and Audrey and Randy Shaneyfelt, who first heard God's call to capture the Healing House story. This book represents the fruit of their obedience.

ABOUT HEALING HOUSE

Our faith-based recovery homes in the Kansas City metro area provide spiritual growth, emotional stability, and direction to prepare men and woman on their journey from addiction while seeking a purposeful life in our community.

Since Healing House's founding in 2003, over 2,000 clients have passed through our doors. Many of these people were homeless upon arrival, 85 percent have been incarcerated, and 40 percent claim to have been raised in an unstable family environment. Even with such odds stacked against them, we're proud to state that over 80 percent of Healing House clients report living addiction-free, productive lives.

Through education and employment training programs and required community service, we are helping to break down barriers to employment including incarceration, tarnished records, scarcity of lower level jobs, and minimal work experience. We eagerly work towards the completion of our multipurpose facility that will offer on-the-job training and work experience, improved recovery support services for individuals in recovery, and generate finances to create a self-sustaining Healing House.

We recognize the disease of addiction as tri-fold: physical, emotional, and spiritual. Our faith-based recovery homes provide a family setting for clients to let down their guard from the harshness of this world.

We take a holistic approach to battling addiction through individual and group recovery support programs, accountability and mentoring arrangements, and numerous spiritual growth opportunities.

To learn more or to make a tax-deductible donation, go to www.healinghousekc.org

ABOUT THE AUTHOR

Bobbi Jo Reed started drinking and drugging at the age of twelve. Her addiction consumed her for the next 22 years, decades scarred by rape, homelessness, abuse and prostitution. At age 34, her father's death at last moved her to stop drinking. Three years later, in the wake of losing her mother, she gave her life to God and began a true transformation.

Throughout her sobriety, Bobbi Jo found that helping others helped her stay sober while giving her purpose. Bobbi Jo founded Healing House in 2003 to provide a stable home for women, and later men, who like her, needed a safe place to fully recover after leaving substance abuse treatment.

Made in the USA
Las Vegas, NV
07 March 2021

19175989R00075